THE ZEN OF BUSINESS
ACQUISITIONS

THE ZEN OF BUSINESS ACQUISITIONS

THOMAS J. HINE,
CFP®, MBA

NEW DEGREE PRESS

THE ZEN OF BUSINESS ACQUISITIONS

ISBN   978-1-64137-363-0   *Paperback*
        978-1-64137-706-5   *Ebook*

This book is dedicated to my family and the future generations of my family.

Mom, Dad, Amy, Carolyn, Charlotte, and Eric-

For all the lessons you have taught me, all the joy and laughter you have brought me, and how you have reminded me to live in the present and with full awareness.

CONTENTS

INTRODUCTION

BEGINNER'S MIND

Los Angeles, California, 1993

The match was tied one to one, and this third match would decide which team would win, advance to the final round, and possibly go to Japan to compete in the 1994 World Tournament. In team sparring, at least in the Shotokan style of martial arts, there are three individual matches, and the judges total the points of all three matches to determine the winner. I was the third man on my team, and I was nervous because I knew it all rested on me. We were only up by half of a point, five and a half to five. Basically that meant my team had scored one more punch or kick than our opponents had. One second of hesitation or delay on my part would erase that advantage.

My team, comprised of my instructor, me, and another senior student, was in the lead. If I held on to the lead or even tied the match with my opponent, we would win and advance. I was the least experienced member of my team by several years, so I knew I had my work cut out for me. It was go time, and I was very nervous.

The chief judge stood between us, looked left and right, then, with a sweeping motion of his hands, announced, "*Hajime,*" (pronounced huh-ji-may), which is the Japanese word for "begin" or "start." At that moment, you blank out everything around you and focus on your opponent. Your field of vision narrows to a small rectangle that matches the height and width of your opponent. Nothing else matters.

I scored first, a reverse punch to the stomach. All of our techniques, in practice and in competition, are designed to stop one inch before the target, so as not to injure your opponent. It is well understood that if you can get your fist, or the ball of your foot, that close to an opponent without them blocking the technique, that would count for at least half a point. You only get a full point (*ippon*) if your opponent is completely defenseless.

Quickly, my opponent scored three times on me in a matter of thirty seconds, all three were half-point punches. I was way too eager to win the match, and it showed. Now I was behind with only a minute to go. My opponent tried to finish me off, but I snuck in a front kick to his midsection, making the score one and one half to one in his favor. This was going to be down to the wire. I was down by one half of a point with very little time left.

The final thirty seconds was a flurry of punches and kicks, each of us trying to finish off the other and wrap up the match. At the last second, our fists became like two bullets passing each other in opposite directions. The chief judge jumped between us as the timekeeper yelled "*time*," which meant the match was over. I thought I scored on this last exchange, so the match would end in a tie. The chief judge stood back and blew a whistle to indicate the other judges had to give their final decision on who won the match, red or white.

The other four judges, who had chairs around the corners of the match area, held up their flags to denote who they thought was the winner of the last exchange. My opponent had a red sash, and I had no sash, which meant by default I was the white color. Fate was not with me that day.

All four flags indicated red. That meant on the last exchange my opponent was quicker to the target than I was. His final punch won it all. I was devastated. I had given it everything I had and came up short. It was frustrating and demoralizing, but I had to accept he was better that day. I felt bad that I had let my team and my instructor down.

There would be no trip to Japan for the World Tournament in sparring.

It would take a long time for the sting of this defeat to wear off.

* * *

In Chinese philosophy, yin and yang describe contrary or opposite forces that actually can be complementary or inter-connected. My first book (yin), was about defense: defending myself from an external threat (securities arbitration). I used the analogy of self-defense but applied it not to a physical fight but a mental fight, a fight in a courtroom where you battle with wits, witnesses, data, testimony, and instinct.

This book is about the other half of a wealth-management practice: offense (yang). By focusing on acquisitions and moving toward growing the AUM (assets under manage-ment), there is a different attitude. A growth mind-set. By focusing on acquisitions, we add more clients, more rela-tionships, more investment accounts, and more confidence.

In martial arts training, at least in the Shotokan style, we learn many techniques that are both defensive and offensive.

For example, we have been taught that if you block a punch using the correct power, your opponent will feel pain and have less incentive to attack again. Your strong defense becomes your best offense. Conversely, if you have a fast punch, your opponent has to maintain a safe distance from you, so your quick offense puts him on defense. Yin and yang, offense and defense.

Think of this book as a mixture of practical business wisdom on acquisitions suffused with a liberal dose of eastern philosophy and martial arts wisdom that emphasizes the key learning points.

* * *

In March of 2007, I published my first book, *NASD Arbitration Solution: Five Black Belt Principles to Protect and Grow Your Financial Services Practice.* It was a thrill and an honor to publish and present several well-attended speeches around the country. My coauthor, John K. Brubaker, was and is a brilliant writer, and we had an amazing collaboration. The book was about surviving and winning a securities arbitration case in New York City circa 2003.

But something about that book never felt complete.

Something has always felt like it was missing.

The inspiration to write the book came from using the wisdom gained from my thirty years (at that time) of martial arts teaching and training in Shotokan karate as a teaching mechanism for other advisors.

I was defending myself in a court of law, an arbitration hearing, yet it felt much greater than that. I eventually "won" the arbitration, that is, I "won" the right to pay nothing; no damages were awarded to the plaintiff. What a Pyrrhic victory. But despite the pain and agony, I learned a lot in those twenty-one months of hearings, testimony, examinations, and cross-examinations. I was a white belt, a beginner, in the world of securities arbitration. That proved to be an advantage, because I was meticulous with my preparation, sharing everything relevant with my attorney. I wrote about this process to educate other advisors and to help cement the lessons learned for my own benefit as well.

Two ideas that became clearer in hindsight were the concepts of Zen and the beginner's mind. They both applied to my arbitration case. And they apply equally to this book as well. These two principles help form the bedrock of this book.

The Zen and beginner's mind quotes came from Shunryu Suzuki (1904–1971), a famous Japanese monk who helped usher in Zen Buddhism in the US and is well known for founding the first Buddhist monastery outside of Asia. In addition, my karate instructor of thirty years, Sensei Mori, always told us to have a "beginner's mind" even after we advanced to first-degree black belt and beyond.

Sensei Masataka Mori was a world-renowned Shotokan instructor who taught for over fifty-five years, and I am truly grateful for all the years I trained under him. He passed away on September 8, 2018, at the age of eighty-five. I was fortunate to attend his funeral and watched, for the first time and in complete awe, a traditional Buddhist funeral ceremony. It was an experience that I will never forget.

I have included part of his biography at the end of this book for reference. The wisdom shared throughout this book is a combination of his teachings, my own training, and my professional experiences in the financial services industry. My sincere desire is that you gain some great knowledge and insight into the current trends of the mergers and acquisitions (M&A) industry, particularly financial services. And maybe, just maybe, some insight into yourself.

Fast forward to January 2019: I am still training in Shotokan karate (fourth degree black belt) and I have added yoga to my workout schedule. The landscape of financial services has changed, and now I want to focus on acquisitions and succession planning, specifically financial services acquisitions.

This book has a classic yin-yang component when compared to my first book.

That was what was missing, and I hope to provide balance to that story that was put out more than a decade ago.

THE BEGINNER'S MIND

"If your mind is empty, it is always ready for anything, it is open to everything. In the beginner's mind there are many possibilities, but in the expert's mind there are few."

—SHUNRYU SUZUKI

This is equally true in business, and in particular, when I started doing acquisitions fifteen years ago. Every deal is unique, every advisor has a different path, a different story, a different outlook. For example, my very first acquisition was bringing over an RIA (registered investment advisor) from Charles Schwab to my broker-dealer at the time. This was considered unconventional, because the industry has gone the other way over the past decade. More and more firms are moving *from* the independent broker-dealer (IBD) model back to the RIA model.

If I had thought about the industry changes and the direction of the tide, I would never have assumed someone would transfer (sell) their book of business from an RIA to a broker-dealer. That was like swimming upstream. I was a beginner; I didn't know any better. The expert would have said, "Don't waste your time." That knowledge, confidence, and experience launched me to acquire six more firms, all very small with under $75 million of assets, and put me on the right path to continue growing. Now I am looking at firms of $200 million or more in AUM as part of my enhanced acquisition process.

THE TRUE PURPOSE OF ZEN

"The true purpose [of Zen] is to see things as they are, to observe things as they are, and to let everything go as it goes . . . Zen practice is to open up our small mind."

—SHUNRYU SUZUKI

This principle is important to us in life and in acquisitions. Over the years, I was tempted many times to buy a practice or a business, looking sometimes at the wrong things. For example, just because a business is physically located near yours doesn't necessarily mean it is a good strategic fit. Another lesson: don't focus on what the seller *says* but on what he or she *does*. Their actions. As Suzuki explains, "So it is with people: first let them do what they want, and watch them. This is the best policy. To ignore them is not good. That is the worst policy. The second worst is trying to control them. The best one is to watch them, just to watch them, without trying to control them."

This book is full of stories, vignettes, insights, and lessons from several experts in the field, including:

- Ron Carson of Carson Wealth learns from his biggest mistakes on his way to managing $10 billion in AUM.

- David Grau of FP Transitions warns us that we are *not* building sustainable businesses for the next generation.

- Carolyn Armitage of ECHELON Partners discusses the three categories of investment firms.

- Dan Kreuter of Gladstone Group explains the Five Elements of Power that buyers should accrue from a successful acquisition.

- James Hughes of Live Oak Bank reviews the critical aspects of financing and acquisition.

I had to remind myself that the practice and discipline of seeing things as they are, without filters or judgments, remains one of the most important aspects of any business decision. That also includes who you hire, acquire, promote, merge with, or fire. It is a lifelong lesson that benefits all of us.

This same lesson was taught to many black belts by my karate instructor Sensei Mori when we enrolled in his judging seminars. We were training to be judges for local tournaments, and he emphasized that when we judged, we should not "project into the future" what we think that each contestant could accomplish. We were simply to judge them (either their kata or *kumite*) "as they are today." In the present moment. In similar fashion, it is easy for entrepreneurs to dream or fantasize about how an acquisition might help in the future, but what will it do for you today? The goal is to focus on the here and now, what is present and real.

I am excited to share with you the wisdom of many well-known advisors and firms throughout the book. Although these advisors do not practice martial arts (as far as I know), they all demonstrate the same themes and philosophy I have witnessed in my training and used in my wealth management practice throughout my career.

Concepts such as:

- Overcoming countless obstacles

- Never giving up

- Keeping your eyes on the prize even when the odds are stacked against you

Perseverance and persistence are the threads that run through these stories. I am sure many of you have your own stories that you have lived and experienced throughout your career that have defined you and made you successful. A famous Japanese quote says, "We learn little from victory, much from defeat."

I have also included a section called "How to Hack This Book." For those readers who want to jump right to the conclusions or key chapters most relevant to the stage of your career, this section allows you to take the left lane and get there quickly.

"How to Hack This Book" summarizes all the key lessons discussed, shown through a prism of six key aspects of acquisitions:

- Culture

- Valuation

- Client Service

- Perseverance

- Traits of Successful Acquisitions

- Beginner's Mind and the True Purpose of Zen

PART 1

VALUATION

CHAPTER 1

TRUELYTICS—BUSINESS INTELLIGENCE SOFTWARE

———

"Fall down seven times, get up eight."

—JAPANESE PROVERB

I want to share an important story with you about perseverance and persistence. In the M&A world, there are countless stories about individuals and firms that never gave up, never quit, and kept focusing on the long game. Terry Mullen is a great example of this grit and determination.

Terry Mullen is the founder and CEO of Truelytics, and I can safely say that he does not suffer from a lack of confidence or low self-esteem. In fact, he is quite the opposite. Although he is only in the third year of his start-up, with incredible vision, energy, and a great product, he knows his biggest challenge is to get his firm's name out there and to get financial advisors to use his software.

Terry is so confident in his software that when he was talking to one of his biggest competitors (with a track record of over fifteen years), he said, "I told him he should be a client of mine. He should be using my software."

Really? That's like a white belt in karate with only a trimester of experience telling a world sparring champion, "You should see my front kick. It is fast, and I doubt you could block it." As Terry told me with great confidence, "When I get to the decision maker, it's like a hundred-percent success rate because we are able to provide a phenomenal product to both the wealth advisor and the broker-dealer."

Terry is acting exactly the way a CEO should be acting and thinking. He is optimistic, driven, and very smart. His product is an evaluation business intelligence tool for wealth management firms. But things aren't always so easy, especially when you play the long game. He has made small, continuous improvements over his entire career, and he has been patient. This is the Japanese concept of *kaizen*.

Kaizen means "continuous improvement." One step at a time. You focus on the small details and keep making positive changes. Many years ago, when I was in a karate instructor class, Sensei Mori had me focus for one full year on improving one specific punch. I practiced that one punch hundreds of times over those twelve months . . . and Sensei Mori corrected me countless times over that same twelve months. While this concept of *kaizen* is not new, trying to apply it in today's fast-paced, Google-driven world of "I want results now" is more difficult than ever.

Terry had dreamed of starting or running his own business since he was a kid. And lo and behold, only three decades later, he has done that, although he is quick to admit that there were many setbacks along the way.

"From a very early age," he said, "I was always thinking I would be an entrepreneur. I always came up with ideas on different products or services."

In 1982, he was suggesting to friends they should sell bottled water from a vending machine at the gym because the water fountains were dirty and never worked right. They looked at him and said, "Why would anyone ever pay for bottled water?

Don't waste your time. It will never work." Have you ever heard of Dasani? Evian? Fiji water? Check out your nearest vending machine.

That got me thinking.

Fast forward to 2019. We can now use our cell phones to hail a ride in New York City (Uber). Also, it is possible to have your dinner delivered by a complete stranger in a Toyota Corolla from a restaurant you've never dined at (Uber Eats).

Why would anyone pay for that?

Uber went public in May of 2019, but they have been playing the long game for over a decade while making continuous changes along the way. They never gave up, and they keep updating their software and services in order to stay ahead of the competition. They still have many challenges even after going public.

THE EARLY YEARS

Terry had plans to start a company in his twenties, but then he started a family, and as any parent will tell you, "There was never a time that I could do it with raising kids." He has invested in a whole bunch of companies, maybe ten to fifteen that were start-ups, and many of them have not worked out.

"I wish I had done it differently," he said, alluding to all the mistakes, lost opportunities, and financial loss. He lost some money along the way, but not every time. He was patient and persistent.

One investment was a shoe company, SeaVees, that was eventually sold to a British company. Another company sold wine in a patented single-serve wine glass, and at the time, that company got the biggest deal on *Shark Tank* that had ever been offered. He looked at two tech companies and another venture that tried to reinvent parking meter technology. Each time, even with a few successes along the way, there was no pot of gold at the end of the rainbow, but Terry never quit. He kept plugging away. And he made changes as needed.

He started off as a wholesaler in the Rocky Mountain states, calling on financial advisors (such as me) to convince them to offer his product to their clients. For example, it might be a mutual fund, an annuity, or some other investment vehicle designed to help the middle class save for retirement, minimize taxes, or both. That job taught him time-management skills and conflict resolution, since he had adjusted to working with many different personalities.

His career progressed from internal wholesale in 1986 to a promotion in sales management for a major insurance company and eventually to a role as national sales manager at that same company. He then joined Lincoln Financial shortly after they moved their headquarters to his hometown of Philadelphia.

He was patient and saw an opening, which is called *kyo* in martial arts. When you are in a sparring competition, you look for a weakness or an opening for the right time to attack your opponent and maximize your chances of winning. Thus when American Funds spun off the distribution of the American Legacy annuity product, it was Terry who saw the opportunity and grew that business to a $7 billion a year behemoth. Then he became head of sales and ultimately head of national distribution where he oversaw more than seven hundred wholesalers. The journey continued.

THE GREAT FINANCIAL CRISIS

In 2008, Terry and the former CEO of Lincoln moved to Boston to try a repeat performance with a major Canadian insurance company.

He said, "I should write a book about this time period because we literally interviewed with the board of directors on September 14, 2008, and the CFO told me he had just met with the Fed and Lehman Brothers, it was filing for bankruptcy the next morning, and Bank of America was buying Merrill Lynch. This was a crucial moment in Wall Street history, and

I was literally making a career-changing decision right in the middle of the chaos."

After the 2008 crisis, the major Canadian insurance company decided to exit the US market to reduce their risk, and Terry then had to do the unthinkable. He had to make an excruciatingly difficult decision and lay off all the people he hired over the past two years. "It was the worst thing in the world," he said. Many of them had followed him throughout his journey, some through three or four different transitions.

"I had an incredible following. I figured out compensation the right way. I was going to incentivize the right behavior, and I wanted the best wholesalers. I didn't want the lower-tier wholesalers."

He broke with traditional compensation structure and did something very entrepreneurial. "If you were a great wholesaler and really drove sales, your payout with my division actually *increased* as opposed to all the other companies that put caps on them and stuff." As he eloquently put it, "It's like, wait a second, the more you do, you're gonna then reduce their payout. That's when I am starting to actually make money as a wholesaler."

So instead of cutting the payout of successful wholesalers as other firms did, he found a way to increase it. Once again, Terry was playing the long game, even with his employees.

But he still had to lay off every single person, it hurt, and Terry never quit.

He continued his journey with a few more corporate moves, but in 2015, an interesting thing happened. He was asked to come in on an interim basis to help turn American Realty Capital around. Then something else fortuitous happened. He ran into a former colleague that ran a combination of an investment bank and an executive search firm.

THE GENESIS OF TRUELYTICS

This firm had developed some software but didn't know what to do with it. This software performed sophisticated evaluation on wealth management firms, and Terry saw an even brighter future. Here was *kyo* again, the opening, reappearing in his life.

"I thought there was so much more to it that I ended up forming my own company called Truelytics," Terry said. "I raised some money and bought the intellectual property rights from them, then spent two years upgrading the software." The long game had paid off. It turns out all those past mistakes and missteps were not failures but merely training lessons.

When you play the long game, you don't know in advance what mistakes and what lessons will be most valuable. My experience is that you have to follow your moral compass, do the right thing, pursue excellence, and add value along the way. If you keep doing that day in and day out, year in and year out, eventually the strategy pays off.

In martial arts, we often learn the most from tournaments where we experience defeat rather than victory. Sensei Mori, my Japanese karate instructor, had a great saying for this. When he would present trophies to the winners of any tournament, he would say "You won today because no one better showed up to beat you. Don't forget you must keep training for the long term. You must continue to train, to get better."

During his due-diligence period, Terry completed lots of analysis on this software program, like an auditor does, to make sure the program worked properly. Terry demonstrated the software to over twenty people who all basically said the same thing: "I love it. It's unbelievable. You're not charging enough." The price was $795 at the time. His competitors were charging from $5,000 to $20,000 for a similar analysis. For example, he gives the client (advisor) a current valuation of their firm along with 50 KPI (key performance indicators) that he says his competitors do not offer.

Truelytics closed seventeen sales last year to large enterprises, firms like Linsco Private Ledger (LPL), Fidelity, and American Funds. He hit the mother lode, because there are forty thousand firms (not a typo) associated with those enterprises. Terry is very pleased.

"We think we are in a perfect spot in this industry because there is so much transition that is going on and will continue to go on," he said. His clients in the valuation area range from $30 million of AUM to over $5 billion in AUM. A tsunami is coming over the next decade, the largest transfer in the history of wealth management. And Terry and Truelytics are right in the middle of it.

Truelytics recently got a big momentum boost in February of 2019. Truelytics won the 2019 Detroit Blockchain & Fin-Tech Pitchfest. They were the grand prize winner . . . and they are just in time for the upcoming transfer of wealth. Any firm or advisor that understands and positions themselves for this wave will have a tremendous advantage over the competition.

The young kid who dreamed of bottled water almost forty years ago has bottlenecked the competition.

According to Terry's research, there are fewer than seven hundred firms (RIAs) that have over $1 billion of assets that they manage. He continues, "Ten years ago, you could probably count that group on two hands. We are seeing an explosion in that area." Here are the key drivers of this "Great

Migration" that Terry refers to on the Truelytics website: acquisitions and breakaway.

Acquisitions are easy to understand: one firm buys part or all of another firm. The breakaway concept is when an existing team from a large firm like Merrill Lynch, for example, starts off right away with $400–$600 million of assets on the day they start their new firm after "breaking away" from their parent company to form an RIA. There are some legal constraints when these firms break away from a parent company, so having great legal counsel is a must.

So why such a fuss over acquisitions and succession planning and the software that goes along with that analysis? Here is a brilliant insight: Terry stated when a firm ages from five to ten to twenty years, growth continues at a good pace. But from twenty years until about thirty years, the growth slowed or dropped off in every critical category.

After thirty years, the scores and metrics were the highest. Why the difference? Why this hiatus from years twenty to thirty? The firms that dealt with succession saw the increase again in key statistics. The firms that *didn't* deal with succession never saw any substantial growth after year twenty, even though those advisors or firms work for another fifteen to twenty years. Clearly this is a powerful message. If you don't do proper continuity and succession planning, you could *waste* ten years of your working life and build almost no incremental value in your business.

Terry had a shocking statistic to share with me. "Eighty percent of financial advisors or wealth management firms do not have an emergency continuity or succession plan in writing. Think about that for a second. If something happens to the owner, their business will be worth nothing."

Literally thousands of these businesses around the country are in this situation. I have personally witnessed advisors passing on at age seventy-five or eighty, and with no continuity plan in place, their spouse and family received *zero value* for the business. Zero value for thirty or more years of work.

Now you see why valuation is so important. Truelytics will do the valuation for the individual or the firm to establish a value to be paid to the beneficiaries or the heirs of those advisors that have not already sold or merged. Moreover, if you are looking to add a succession partner or buy out an existing partner, you need to know the current value of your firm.

Even with the current success of Truelytics, Terry had one more hill to climb. He had to fire his founding partner last year, who had more of a technology background but added no real corporate value. "He was a complete empty suit, and I didn't know it at first." This was another difficult decision, but Terry was still playing the long game, getting his company ready for the wave of advisors that would need his evaluation software.

After Terry fired that partner and his replacement came in, things have taken off. The company is clearly moving in the right direction. They will be announcing a huge improvement in their valuation software protocol this spring. Instead of answering 103 questions to get a full-blown evaluation, you will be able to answer a mere seven questions and input your zip code to get 24 KPIs (key performance indicators) that relate to your current valuation tied to your geographical area and your cohorts or peer groups. This is like the Kelley Blue Book for financial services practices, and maybe the next generation of software might be like Carvana.

Many firms have pegged the upcoming intergenerational wealth transfer as one of the largest in history. Accenture, my former firm, estimates $30 trillion of intergenerational wealth is about to exchange hands over the coming years. Pershing Advisors estimates that the wealth management industry will need to add almost 250,000 new advisors over the next decade just to maintain current support levels.

Terry's firm, Truelytics, calls this the Great Transition. I call it the Transition Tsunami.

KEY ACTION STEPS/TAKEAWAYS

1. Continuous improvement (*kaizen*) is a philosophy that should be studied and implemented.

2. Confidence is key. When you know you have a good idea or product to share, don't be shy about sharing.

3. Continuity plans are rare. Eighty percent of advisors don't have a well-thought-out, vetted written plan.

CHAPTER 2

BLIND LEADING
THE BLIND

———

"I fear not the man who has practiced ten thousand kicks once, but I fear the man who has practiced one kick ten thousand times."

—BRUCE LEE

I am quite sure by now that most if not all of you have heard the expression "practice makes perfect." Whether it is music, sports, chess, or even a national spelling bee, it is universally accepted that those who practice diligently and with focus have a good chance of becoming proficient at something. The same is true in the M&A business. The key question any white belt or beginner would ask is "Practice what?"

For starters, all of us need to know what our current "practice" is worth. Regardless if you are buying, selling, merging, or simply want something for your estate-planning attorney to mull over, the bottom line is you start where you are now. The present moment, as a Zen practitioner might say.

Your next question might be "Well, who is good at valuing my practice? Who knows how to do this well?" I would start with someone who has practiced diligently for many years with a good degree of success.

If you were to use a martial arts analogy, I would want a seasoned black belt to thoroughly evaluate my business—at least for firms under $250 million in assets. In my opinion, that black belt is David Grau Sr. of FP Transitions. David is one of the original founders of FP Transitions and is the current president. He was a former securities regulator and securities attorney. He has spent virtually half his life in the industry, helping advisors set up their practices, rearrange them, value them, tweak them, sell them, and everything in between.

David is the author of the best-selling *Succession Planning for Financial Advisors: Building an Enduring Business* published by Wiley & Sons in 2014. His second book, *Buying, Selling, and Valuing Financial Practices: The FP Transitions M&A Guide*, was published in 2016. These two books provide the foundation for most advisors as they consider what to do with their life's work, whether it is retirement or other exit strategies. Among his various awards, he was honored to be on the 2017 *InvestmentNews* list of icons and innovators.

One of David's most important quotes is a brilliant twist on a buyer ultimately thinking like a seller.

Over the course of a career, every single advisor we talk to at some point or another needs to think like a buyer. Toward the end of the career, every single advisor needs to start thinking like a seller.

This is yet another application of the yin-yang concept; apparently opposite sides of the coin are really one and the same. In my thirty years as an investment advisor, we are often taught at seminars to make sure our employees "think like an owner." But we as owners are also taught to "think like an employee" so we understand and appreciate how our employees view their work and their career. As I said in my introduction, thinking like a beginner, "beginner's mind," allows you to have a fresh perspective and prevents your practice from getting stale. Remember, in the beginner's mind there are many possibilities.

David goes on to say that owners must pass those responsibilities of running the firm to the next generation. The Achilles heel of our industry is "sustainability"; in fact, he flat out states, "Our industry is *not* building sustainable businesses. Every year we [at FP Transitions] get to create two hundred to three hundred first-time, next-generation owners, but it's a drop in the bucket when you consider there are about three hundred thousand independent advisors comprised of registered reps (RR), registered investment advisors (RIAs), and independent insurance agents."

Clearly, a lot of beginners out there have not begun the continuity or succession-planning part of their business. They have not begun playing the long game.

David and his firm have done over ten thousand valuations over the last fifteen years, small to large and young to old, the whole gamut. Clearly, in Bruce Lee's words, he has "practiced" diligently throughout those ten thousand valuations, and the lessons learned are crucial. I should know. David worked personally on my first acquisition in September of 2004, and it has been one of my best acquisitions that keeps paying dividends each year. David breaks these practices into three categories or distinct sectors: those who own a book, those who own a practice, and those who own a business. The valuation difference is obvious: Owning a sustainable business is far better than owning a "book of business."

Jeanie O'Reilly Northcutt is one of the original employees at FP Transitions. How she met David was accidental. She was a single mom raising two children on her own, working part-time for a chiropractor when one of the patients introduced her to David Grau and said that David needed a legal assistant. So she became his legal assistant during his days as an attorney when he was doing menial U4 and U5 work and was one of the first people with whom he shared his vision about an "online marketplace for advisors" who want to buy or sell their practices. She would often ask him early on, "What is it we do again? What is this thing with the website?"

As she tells the story, one of the original five founding partners initially thought they would just build this website and people would go online and meet each other without much interaction; you might call this a matchmaker for investment advisors. As time went on, they were stunned at how much interaction the advisors needed. In her words, "The advisors needed guidance, help, coaching, coaxing, and confidence to complete these complex transactions." In short, they needed practice.

This process of merging, acquiring, or selling involves many steps. Just as David has practiced over ten thousand valuations, you too have to practice at getting your company ready to sell or merge. And this requires years of planning, from deciding on what business model to offer (fee, retainer, or transaction), what type of staff to hire (administrative only or CFP associates), and what marketing campaigns to run (organic or acquisition-oriented). Also, you must decide whether to have salaried CFP advisors or those that share in the revenue (split rep code) of each client. In addition, you have to have a great contact-management system (Redtail or Junxure) that allows you to save and retrieve client data efficiently.

Along the way, you might have to make changes, modify your tactics, and even be prepared to throw out the current playbook. After the 2008–2009 financial crisis, I changed the entire way that my firm manages money, which meant that almost everything I had been taught since 1990 was karate-chopped out of existence. I could not resist the pun! Seriously though, you have to be prepared to start over, rethink your current goals and objectives, and make sure you are on track for the long term. There are many great coaching programs that can help. I can think of two that have helped me tremendously: Dan Sullivan's Strategic Coach and Ron Carson's Excel program. If you have not researched these programs, go online and see what these programs are all about. Online search engines are the de facto standard to help you acquire knowledge and put it to work instantly.

Networking has become the preferred choice for the small advisors to sell: many smaller firms are now being bought or sold directly without FP Transitions, with new buyers and new sellers connecting on their own using social media, conventions, seminars, local FPA meetings, etc. Most advisors don't have a succession plan, and as they get older, they are treading water. The book of business declines in value as their clients get older, and they don't market to grow their firm. They need help to create the succession plan to sell their practice while it is still valuable. As Jeanie says, "The first step is to get a valuation, and it's all about the fit. It's all about finding the buyer that will take care of the clients like you did. A lot of predatory buyers out there are taking advantage of older sellers, and they don't know if the buyer may change the book of business around or cherry-pick the best clients and ignore all the other clients after the sale is done."

She has some great words of wisdom for new buyers: *"Don't sign offer sheets until they are looked over by a competent lawyer."* In one case, a seller was duped into selling a practice when they thought they were signing a simple continuity plan, a "practice emergency plan," as Jeanie said. It turns out the document basically said, "No matter what, you are selling your practice." This is ironic that at the same time the industry regulators are worried about "senior abuse" or "elder abuse" with the general financial-investing public, that the same thing is happening to elder financial advisors. Therefore, you have a wave of new first-time buyers (beginners) interacting with first-time sellers. As Jeanie states, "It's like the blind leading the blind." In martial arts, we never had green or brown belts teaching white belts. We always had experienced second- or third-degree black belts doing the teaching because they had the knowledge, wisdom, and experience.

So the best analogy to our industry would be for many of you who are beginners to start attending webinars, listening to podcasts, attending conferences, and reading. And continue doing this each week or quarterly so that you get familiar with the trends, the terms, and the techniques. Get to know what critical aspects of your business, the metrics, need monitoring and improving. Learn some of the new planning software that integrates with your asset allocation models. You must start to find out what your company is worth. And you should focus on what makes it more profitable and more appealing to a buyer.

Their first step is always to recommend a valuation. Jeanie says FP Transitions gets caught in the middle because they cannot give legal advice to one side over the other, all they can do is give guidance to both sides equally. They always tell advisors the first step is to get a valuation.

"Sellers and buyers have to be realistic. When one side gets greedy, it just doesn't work out well."

Both sellers and buyers would be wise to read many books and attend several seminars on these topics of mergers, acquisitions, and exit strategies. That way, they can become more like a black belt by planning for the long term and becoming an expert in their own ecosystem.

SELLERS' CHECKLIST

Selling to a firm two to three times your size has advantages and disadvantages:

1. The big advantages are that the likelihood of getting paid typically grows with the size of the acquirer, and the technology might be more advanced.

2. The big drawbacks are that your clients might not fit the typical profile of the larger firm, and your clients might be assigned less experienced advisors.

Sellers have to be aware of the following common concerns:

- What is the culture of your firm compared to the firm you want to sell to?

- Are the clients of both firms similar? Are they white-collar and professional or blue-collar and hourly?

- Does the buyer's firm have the same business model? RIA or IBD or hybrid?

- What does the fee structure look like compared to your current model?

- Does your firm create fee-based financial plans? What software is used? What about the acquiring firm?

- Is the client service model similar to your current model?

- Is the staffing mostly administrative or are they CFP professionals?

Typical sellers are in their sixties now, but the "magic number is always five years," according to Jeanie. That is, every advisor that *should* sell, no matter their age, always says "in five years I will be ready to sell." So the new trend is sellers stay on to work while they are transitioning the practice. Jeanie says the female sellers are wiser, they often get out younger and pursue other careers while the men stay on longer and don't know what they will do with their time (she laughs nervously as she shares this story). The men feel "if they stop working they are going to die . . . It's really sad." They think if they stop, they have "given up on life. They don't have other things to do." She continues, "It's ironic that an advisor spends their whole life advising clients about retirement but do little or none of this for themselves."

Bottom line: you need to start practicing for your next chapter in life. In Shotokan karate, it often takes ten years to become a fifth-degree black belt, the level at which you are called an expert, on your way to being a master. In those ten years, you have done thousands of kicks, punches, blocks, and strikes. You need a long-term plan. You need to start with a valuation. Then you have to keep practicing, getting better each year, refining and improving your processes.

You want to plan for the long term and become an expert, a black belt, at your own succession plan.

KEY ACTION STEPS/TAKEAWAYS

1. You should create a ten-year plan for succession and start today by focusing on the team you have now. If your team today is not the one you had in mind, then start building your new team.

2. You must practice diligently at growing, strengthening, and evaluating your firm. Look at industry-comparable statistics for firms your size as a starting point. Start reading books, attending seminars, and browsing white papers.

3. You should pay a competent firm to do an evaluation of your company as soon as possible.

PART 2

ACQUISITIONS / CONSULTING

CHAPTER 3

CAR WASHES, CONGLOMERATES, AND CUISINE

———

"One must be deeply aware of the impermanence of the world."

—DOGEN, *A PRIMER OF SOTO ZEN*

What do car washes, conglomerates, and cuisine have in common? Actually, they have a fourth *C* in common: the consumer. And in the current economic environment, the first three are all heavily involved in the M&A business. These days around the United States and the world, there are many stories of successful companies growing through acquisitions. Many of these acquisitions involve getting greater market share to cater to an ever-changing consumer.

In this chapter, I will focus on three different industries that deal with the changing needs of the consumer. I chose three unrelated businesses to demonstrate the pervasiveness of the M&A activity today regardless of the industry. Moreover, I chose these industries because I think readers can easily relate to car washes, conglomerates, and cuisine.

According to a report by Ernst & Young, "Ten years ago, boardrooms were paralyzed by uncertainty. Today they are motivated by uncertainty . . . A record number of executives are now looking to transact M&A business in the next twelve months."

They are all focusing on the long game. They are reinventing their future, as the Ernst & Young report says, by "learning from the past while envisioning the future in a digitally enabled, hyper-speed world." Things are changing and changing fast.

CAR WASHES

Which brings me to car washes. Car washes might seem a bit old-school, non-digital, nontechnical, and outdated, but the smart money knows this business is far from washed up. Over the years, I have had many conversations with the owner of my local car wash. He has shared many insights with me about the cycle of the business, and he has always played for the long term. I often see Mike at the car wash, but I also frequently run into him at the yoga studio in town.

If you want to know how I met Mike, you can thank the allergy season in New England. For many years, I would often visit his car wash to get the tree pollen and sap off my car. Because I am very sensitive to tree pollen and ragweed, in order to mitigate my allergic reaction, I wanted to minimize my exposure to specific allergens. I'll admit I was a bit obsessive, because if we had a bad pollen season, I would find myself going through his car wash more than once a week. He and the team of employees were always cheerful and pleasant when they greeted me.

Mike is in his mid-sixties, of medium height, has reddish curly hair, and is muscular and wiry at the same time. This September, he will celebrate fifty years in the car wash business. Yes, you did the math right. He started working at age twelve for Consolidated Cigar Company in Connecticut, then at the ripe old age of fourteen made a career change. Mike made a very important choice in his life. He started working in the car wash business at fourteen and never stopped. So if there is *anyone* that knows about business cycles and long-term sustainability, Mike gets my vote.

Recently he spotted a RFID electronic tag on the top left corner of my windshield as my car entered the wash, and he asked me some specific questions. He mostly wanted to know about my car wash experience, the price I was paying, and the level of service I received. Then I asked him if he knew about the acquisitions (also known as "rollups") going on in his line of work. Sure enough, he told me to do some research on Palladin. That simple RFID tag led me to a great story.

Palladin Consumer Retail Partners (Palladin), originally known as Palladin Capital Group, is a Boston-based private investment firm founded in 1998 that focuses mainly on the retail and consumer product sectors. Palladin might not be a household name, but you might know some of their investment holdings, both current and prior. Restoration Hardware, Inmotion Entertainment, and Spencer's are just a few of the companies they have worked with over the past fifteen years.

The principals of Palladin have invested in, financed, or managed over a hundred public and private companies in the consumer product space. Their sweet spot are those retail and consumer product companies that have revenues in the range of $50 million to $500 million. Palladin typically seeks to invest 10–15 percent of equity capital in each transaction, but they have access to deeper pockets through their investment partners if the situation warrants it.

Palladin Consumer Retail Partners LLC made a big splash in the M&A business when they acquired Greenwich, Connecticut–based Splash Car Wash, a regional operator of car washes on November 5, 2018. Goldman Sachs Specialty Lending Group provided the debt financing for the transaction and a revolving credit facility to support future growth. Splash Car Wash was founded in 1981 and is a well-known regional operator of car washes with eighteen locations in New York and Connecticut. Splash built their brand by offering several options such as full service, handwash, express, and self-service alternatives. Interestingly, they also offered oil and lube services at some of their premier locations. Splash provides its customers (consumers) with several options and adds an interesting twist in offering monthly subscriptions and à la carte pricing.

Some of the original businesses to use monthly subscription fees were mail-order book clubs, cable TV, and health clubs. The newer business model, popularized by Netflix and others, is the monthly subscription fee with à la carte pricing. Car washes have joined this revolution. The monthly subscription is done using a digitally enabled RFID tag. So in my case, although I used another well-known competitor, the same scenario applies. I can go as many times a month as I want to have my car washed, in the automated line only, for $29.95 a month.

Compare those concepts with fee-only planners and other firms who are moving away from the AUM (assets under management) model and toward the monthly planning fee or subscription fee model. You can also add flat-fee or fixed-fee planning as an alternative to the AUM model. Change is everywhere.

Mike shares some great wisdom when he opines this monthly subscription model, at least as it applies to car washes. In his opinion, it is oversold and it leads to higher overhead. Mike made another choice to focus on only his one car wash and not expand into multiple locations. He cites a friend of his who owns a car wash in Massachusetts and compares the volume and expenses of that car wash against his cousin's numbers:

> My friend earned $2 million in revenue washing 250,000 cars, and my cousin who owns a similar-size car wash in Rhode Island earned $1 million in revenue washing just 50,000 cars a year. And the overhead with those monthly tags is much higher.

You might think automation is the answer, but even the touchless (automated) car wash needs to be replaced. Mike cites an example of a ten-year-old touchless machine that needs to be replaced for $250,000, and yet it still does not clean the cars as well as the one that uses manual labor.

More locations mean more equipment, more machines, and more headaches.

The overhead costs can also be significant when you acquire another RIA or wealth management firm. Most new acquirers vastly underestimate the expenses of rent, staffing, existing bonus structures, and client service models. I turned down many potential deals because of these prior costs, sometimes called "legacy costs" in the technology world. Many years ago, one large firm with over $200 million in AUM wanted me to bring on one of their employees as a partner. This was a disguised way of selling his firm to his junior partner using my money. That deal was six feet under even before the appetizers arrived for lunch.

Mike explained with animated hand gestures as he pointed at various spots around his car wash. "Look, when you have the monthly subscription fee, it creates an incentive to get people to come through more often. I get that. But your costs go up a lot; soap for example"—he jabbed a finger in the direction of his storage area—"you have to order tons of soap to clean 250,000 cars. And then there is maintenance on all the moving parts. The more cars you bring through, the more often the machinery breaks down." Mike shared with me that starting with raw land, the overall cost to put in a competitive car wash facility is around $5 million. The annual maintenance and upkeep, not including payroll, is well into six figures.

As Mike summarizes, "They don't ever learn, these new buyers that come into our business every decade or so. They keep kicking the can down the road, waiting for profitability, but they don't learn from others' mistakes." He thinks that will happen again. Mike has seen this story before, where these new firms come in and overpay for a car wash business, then they end up selling to someone else years later at a lower price.

CONGLOMERATES

Speaking of lower prices, let's switch gears to the summer of 1930, at the beginning of the Great Depression. Times were tough, prices were low, and jobs were in short supply. Elton Bryson Stephens sold magazines that summer door-to-door in order to pay for his college education at Birmingham-Southern College. He learned from an early age that he had a special talent—he could sell. He could relate to the consumer. He later named the company after his initials, Elton B. Stephens Company, and thus it became EBSCO. It was later renamed to EBSCO Industries Inc. to better reflect all the different companies that were under one corporate roof.

In 1944, he set his sights on a big dream. He made a choice, a conscious one. He was playing the long game, looking well into the future. He and his wife Alys formed a partnership. Their first business was a magazine service that sold subscriptions: their customer was the United States Army. That partnership, seventy-five years later, would become one of the largest privately held companies in the United States. As of 2019, they have over six thousand employees worldwide and over twenty-five distinct businesses under the heading of EBSCO Industries Inc. Their strategy, almost from the beginning, was to grow through acquisitions. EBSCO is the quintessential conglomerate.

EBSCO forged their future in the 1970s and 80s when the corporate mantra was to diversify your holdings and acquire businesses that may *not* be related to your core business. This theory is similar to what financial advisors do when they allocate money across different asset classes that are non-correlated. Basically, non-correlated means they don't move up and down at the same time. The goal of this diversification is simple. You want the earnings and cash flows from the various businesses to help offset each other during difficult economic and business environments.

This mantra of diversification was a prominent theory for most of corporate America during those two decades. In martial arts, we often train with other instructors from the different parts of the world, because this diversification by style can teach us new interpretations of the same techniques or even new techniques entirely. I even recall training under a guest Judo instructor who showed us grappling techniques we had never seen before. This diversification enhanced our learning and understanding of martial arts. Like EBSCO, we were diversifying to grow.

If you get a chance to browse the EBSCO website, they have two key phrases that resonate within their culture.

"Excellence in all we do" and "create positive results." Moreover, the website summarizes the current EBSCO Industries this way:

> EBSCO is a diverse organization with many businesses, but we operate as one company. Our success has been created by our commitment to a shared set of principles. We are an entrepreneurial organization that is driven to grow. We are committed to our future, our communities, and realizing our full potential—collectively and individually.

One major division, EBSCO Information Services, focuses on selling products and services to libraries of all types, schools, and the education market around the world. One of the major players inside that division is Mark Herrick, a senior vice president. The company has grown twenty-fold to about $1 billion in sales over the past twenty years. Their track record of over sixty-three acquisitions, with only a few failures along the way, is an amazing batting average. They created a great systematic process of acquisitions and kept refining it over the past twenty years. They never took short-cuts, and they were patient. They continued to focus on their end user, the consumer.

One of the very few failures they experienced early on was a business project called Currency. The Currency project was an acquisition that would allow them to diversify into the guidance department and career information services area, focusing on the high school marketplace. From a strategic view, it seemed like a no-brainer: EBSCO could gain a foot-hold in local libraries and local schools. Because they had already sold some products in this space and had some prior connections, it seemed a natural fit.

What went wrong? Three key aspects were on a collision course soon after the deal was completed.

First, the marketing and sales organization did not fully appreciate how difficult it would be to sell to a different audi-ence. A different consumer. The library staff, where EBSCO had already sold prior products and established strong rela-tionships, was a great starting point, but they were not the key decision makers. As it turned out, the guidance departments and the superintendent's office were the key players in this game. The sales team was not able to penetrate this different set of new buyers effectively.

Second, product support was not able to navigate the new complexities of additional services. The product team already knew how to manage and position large collections of research to libraries, but Currency contained some additional services. Currency included assessments, tracking functions, and integrations with other student systems. Communication of the key benefits of these new features posed new challenges and proved difficult to translate to the market. The lack of expertise in the career guidance area was a drawback to creating fast, responsive solutions for the customer.

Last but not least was the technology angle. The product was written in an older language called Cold Fusion, and EBSCO had effectively no employee that knew that programming language. They did keep one employee from the acquisition that knew Cold Fusion, but they ended up contracting out most of the work. The technology people became annoyed with this Cold Fusion thing ("Why did we ever buy this product anyway? No one uses this language anymore."). Sales started off slow, and you know how this story ends. The Currency project never got the priority, attention, and funding it needed to succeed. Thus, Currency closed down and some of the content was transferred to another product line.

Over the past fifteen years, EBSCO refined their acquisition process to weed out the possibility of another disappointing project like Currency. For example, they constantly reinforced what I call the "great Monday morning–after feeling." EBSCO wanted the sellers of any company to feel the same way coming into work the Monday after a deal was closed. They consciously want all the new employees of the acquired firm to feel just as good the next week about the company and their own job as they did right before the company was sold. They would put more emphasis on how things would integrate the next week and how all the pieces would fit together based upon more in-depth technical and market-based research.

Their CEO, Tim Collins, clearly wanted all future acquisitions to focus on integration, how things fit together, how EBSCO made it easy for the end user. They made conscious choices moving forward. One of the recent quotes on their philosophy is:

> Simply put, the universe within which EBSCO's discovery and access tools operate expands beyond our own servers. Customers are wanting seamless access and single sign-on for their users to access content no matter where that content resides.

The fourth C, the consumer, the customer, makes its appearance again.

Another big change they made was adding business brokers to the acquisition process. This twist produced an interesting by-product. While EBSCO could have continued going it alone (they already had an exceptional process), adding the business broker opened them up to new opportunities they would otherwise have missed.

More importantly, in two cases, EBSCO knew the seller well in advance of using a business broker. However, it was the *seller* who requested the services of the business broker because it made them feel more protected and more secure in the deal. I have experienced the exact same scenario in the financial services acquisition market. When the seller is inexperienced or feels overwhelmed, the use of a competent business broker can help navigate the twists and turns of a sale or merger. In fact, this is *exactly* what happened when my firm bought out Mike Hurst, as you will read in Chapter 9.

What were the benefits of using a business broker with the seller? One key reason is due diligence. When EBSCO works with the seller's business broker, the broker's job is to cull through all the data the seller has, filter out the noise and the extraneous details, and focus on the key accounting and sales numbers. Mark explains one classic technique that sellers use to beef up the purchase price: unrealistic sales projections. The industry term is "hockey stick sales projections."

Mark explains, "the seller has an incentive to really want to crank up these future sales numbers, because the seller often gets paid, at least in part, on how well the company grows *after* the acquisition is complete. If you have ever seen these charts in a presentation, they look flat—horizontal for a while—then boom, after the acquisition, they leap upward to the right, forming what looks like a hockey stick." Mark and his team know that a good business broker will scrutinize these details and projections long before an offer is made.

Another tactic that can be used in private companies is to pay big bonuses or special dividends to key personnel after due diligence is complete but before the deal is signed. Therefore, large sums of money that the acquiring company thought might be available have already been spent. In other words, the seller uses time to their advantage. I would call this tactic "time arbitrage." This can happen in any industry at any time. Buyer beware.

EBSCO solved the "time arbitrage" problem a long time ago. They have always had a sense of urgency and secrecy when they do their acquisitions. Their solution is elegant and simple. They structure the due diligence and the closing in a very short window of time. Mark told me it is not uncommon to be finalizing due diligence and editing contract language twenty-four to thirty-six hours before closing. Therefore, there is no time delay to take advantage of.

EBSCO Industries has succeeded by playing the long game and taking the time to allow each acquisition to flourish. If you peruse their website, they now have the following portfolio of companies:

Information Services

CINAHL

EBSCO Information Services

EBSCO LearningExpress

GOBI Library Solutions from EBSCO

NoveList

Publishing and Digital Media

152 Media

Consumer Subscription Services

EBSCO Professional Partnership Group

Publishers' Warehouse

Manufacturing and Distribution

All Current Electrical Sales

EBSCO Sign Group

IMAGEN Brands

Luxor

PRADCO Outdoor Brands

Vulcan Industries

Real Estate

Alys Beach

EBSCO Income Properties

The Town of Mt Laurel

Insurance Services

Valent Group

CUISINE

Quiz question. What industry today has sales of $17 billion, is expected to grow to $60 billion to $80 billion in 2022, and is still largely unprofitable?

Answer: Online grocery sales.

There is fierce competition between grocers, restaurants, and supermarkets to grow as fast as possible, even with no clear path to profits in the near future. They are all chasing the fourth C, the almighty consumer. At this moment, no one brand is winning this war of attrition. Impermanence is everywhere.

Although the number of deals has slowed recently, funding is up globally for all of these third-party restaurant and grocery store delivery services since 2016. Just like with financial services and car washes, there is plenty of money to go around, which increases the cutthroat nature of this business.

In addition to Amazon, companies like SoftBank Group Corp, T. Rowe Price Group Inc., and Fidelity Management & Research Company have used their deep pockets to fund start-ups like Deliveroo. Deliveroo is a UK–based food delivery company that currently works with eighty thousand restaurant and takeout outlets globally.

Today, the major players in this cuisine-to-order market (as I call it) are DoorDash, Uber Eats, Grubhub, Postmates, and

Caviar. These companies are what are called "third-party platforms" for the restaurant business. If you add in Blue Apron and HelloFresh and several other smart competitors, the choices can be overwhelming. And the profits are underwhelming.

This business model reminds me of the robo-advisors that have tried to take over the investment world. These robo-advisors offer virtual guidance on your finances based on algorithms, and can be done without the face-to-face meetings with a traditional financial advisor. While the industry just passed its tenth anniversary, it remains to be seen if this will continue to be a viable solution, given some of the technology challenges and glitches some firms have experienced during volatile markets. The next bear market will provide an excellent case study to determine the profitability and responsiveness of this model. Stay tuned.

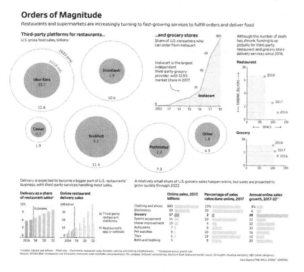

Orders of Magnitude
Restaurants and supermarkets are increasingly turning to fast-growing services to fulfill orders and deliver food.

Profits to Go

Delivery and packaging fees take a big cut of restaurant profits, and deliveries often don't include beverages, which provide high margins.

■ Ribs and a salad   ■ Beverage
■ In-unit labor   ■ Packaging   ■ Delivery fee

Served on premises

Total check $30.00

Cost   9.25

Profit: $20.75
(69% of total check)

Delivered via third party

Total check $25.00

Cost   15.38

Profit: $9.63
(39% of total check)

Note: Food margin is 67%, compared to 85% for beverages. Packaging cost is 3.5% of total check; delivery fee: 25% of total check.

Source: Pentallect

Instacart is currently the largest independent third-party grocery provider with almost a 13 percent market share in 2017. Their tagline is "groceries in as little as one hour." Their web page also mentions stores they partner with locally, and in my area, it showed the logos and names of ALDI, PriceRite, Total Wine, and Costco.

Almost every major player in this industry is truly playing the long game. Many are going through an epic acquisition binge, the grocery equivalent to watching all *Game of Thrones* and *Walking Dead* episodes over a summer break! They are making conscious choices about where to expand and with whom and how to make it work. And it is not easy.

Walmart bought Jet.com for $3.3 billion in 2016, but including the dozen or so other third-party delivery partners, they still expect e-commerce losses to increase in the 2019 fiscal year.

An online grocery service, Shipt, was acquired by Target for $550 million in 2017. John Mulligan, COO of Target, says "I'll be honest, it's not easy. From a pure relevance standpoint, you have to figure it out, because that's how shoppers are going to interact with you." Again, the consumer, the fourth *C*, is onstage again.

Amazon bought Whole Foods in 2017 for a whopping $13.7 billion. More amazing was that the actual value of Whole Foods's current operation was only valued at approximately $4 billion, which leaves the goodwill (future growth value) portion of the purchase price at $9 billion. Amazon continues to demonstrate its focus on delivering all sorts of consumer goods, from furniture to finger food, right to the doorstep of the consumer. However, Amazon does not always win. In a USA Today snippet from June 24, 2019, Amazon announced it was ending its meal delivery service in the US. The reason? Fierce competition from rivals Grubhub, Uber Eats, and DoorDash.

Restaurants can't ignore the delivery game, whether they want to or not.

Recent data suggests nearly a third of restaurant meals are consumed at home, up 2 percent from the previous year ending in September. Contrast that with the dine-in sales volume, which has been flat over the same period of time. This explains why the industry is willing to spend so much money without seeing profits: companies are not seeing much growth inside their stores, so they have to reach out to the consumer [customer] directly.

DOWNLOAD, CLICK, OR CALL

So where does that leave us, the customer, the consumer? Considering all the choices we have now, how do we know the best option? I am sure the vast majority of us want healthy food at a great low price that is restaurant-quality and delivered right to our front door. And in many cases, families still enjoy the healthy aspect of cooking together. I know my family has enjoyed cooking and sharing a great meal from one of those well-known meal-delivery companies.

One answer that may help the consumer is the same concept that helped create this maze of choices: technology. It will become increasingly important for consumers (the fourth C) to make intelligent choices about the technology they use to sort through an array of choices. Using today's technology, you can download an app and order quality food within minutes. At your office computer, you can go to your favorite restaurant's website and click on a to-go order. And last but not least, you can always call the old-fashioned way and talk to a live person to place your takeout order.

Because of the impermanence in the world, change is a constant. The consumer is changing, technology is changing, and the competition is changing.

This is a constant cycle that will produce winners and losers, and that in of itself will create more change.

KEY ACTION STEPS/TAKEAWAYS

1. Acknowledge the impermanence of the world and adapt to these challenges. Make this a conscious part of your overall acquisition process.

2. Accept that acquisitions are happening everywhere. Learn what you can from other industries, as the concepts often apply to financial services acquisitions.

3. Anticipate what your competitors will do in different scenarios. Amend your strategy accordingly.

CHAPTER 4

ACQUISITION MANIA

"Three things cannot be long hidden: the sun, the moon, and the truth."

—GAUTAMA BUDDHA

Many of the challenges in business, indeed in life, revolve around getting to the truth. The same could be said of the stock market. One classic question investors ask is "What is the true value of this stock?" when trying to form a conclusion about buying or selling a security. The same logic clearly applies to the M&A business. Oftentimes we hear about valuation, multiples, gross revenues, and other technical terms without acknowledging one simple fact: these are all tools at getting at the truth, the true value of a company, an entity, or a conglomerate.

This is why I want to introduce you to Dave DeVoe. DeVoe is indeed one of the rock stars of the M&A business. Some of his insights are obvious, others are truly insightful and worth their weight in gold. He is well recognized in the valuation part of the M&A business, especially at the larger end of the asset scale where all the trends are being defined and refined.

If you were to meet Dave DeVoe in person (I have not), you might think he looks like an investment banker or M&A type right out of Berkley; in fact, he looks the part exactly. That's because he is. He has a warm and friendly smile with close-cropped hair and round glasses. He founded his name-sake firm in 2011 to help wealth management companies optimize their business decisions. Dave has been focused on RIA practice management for almost two decades and was recently called an "RIA M&A Guru" by *Barron's* magazine. He has worked with hundreds of firms in the valuation and consulting services since he launched his firm DeVoe & Company. They love how their clients describe them: Rock stars. Thought leaders. Nerds. Therapists with spreadsheets (my favorite). The truth is that DeVoe & Company is well-known and very capable.

DeVoe & Company has a big challenge ahead. Thousands of advisors across the country have three major headwinds that DeVoe has to overcome. First, they are all growing older and by and large are resistant to change and slow to move. Second, the transition issues are both very emotional and highly technical. Third, the intensity of competition has forced firms to merge, sell, or adapt at a much more rapid pace than was historically necessary.

In a 2017 interview, DeVoe laid out some amazing statistics about the industry and the true level of M&A activity. While he and his peers have seen record levels, quarter after quarter of increasing activity, he shares an astute observation about what's not happening. *DeVoe says, "This is a hyper-fragmented industry with ten thousand-plus firms when we are seeing only one to two hundred transactions per year."* Given the industry demographics, he expects to see continued increases over the next five years. The reality is the average age of the owner or founder of most firms is nearing sixty. This is an obvious challenge for the industry, and it is not rocket science; more and more advisors will have to create succession plans over the next decade.

DeVoe & Company's smallest client has $40 million in assets, the largest client has over $60 billion. The ideal target for them, the "sweet spot," is anywhere from $200 million to $2 billion in assets. As he assesses the changes in the marketplace, DeVoe says that "years ago, it was all about having control of the business, and now the M&A activity is more about the scale and off-loading some of the complexities of compliance and operations."

So what is stopping advisors from entering the fray and executing a merger or acquisition? DeVoe says only 30 percent of advisors have a succession plan in place. DeVoe has a theory that once advisors start to look at all the steps involved, they can get overwhelmed and confused, so they delay the decision. They "kick it off another quarter or two quarters." His firm recently developed SuccessionWorks to help smooth out this process. It is comprised of over thirty modules, and his firm helps you determine what pieces you already have in place and weaves them together with those you will need. The reality is that for beginners, the M&A business is complicated and can seem overwhelming at times. Learning new valuation software along with absorbing accounting, tax, and staffing modifications can be a daunting task. If you add in pension plans, 401(k) plans, and estate tax law, you can easily see why advisors choose to look the other way and keep working.

In some cases, an older or seasoned advisor has challenges finding the right advisor, the right fit, to take over his firm. In other cases, the talent is not in-house, or even if the talent is in-house, they cannot afford to purchase the firm because it got so successful and valuable. Sometimes, the advisors just don't want to retire; they have no other hobbies. Quotes like "they're going to carry me out in a box" or "I'm going to die with my boots on" are not uncommon in this business. The truth is that thousands of older advisors someday have to sell or exit the business. Just like the sun and the moon, we can pretend to look the other way, but we cannot hide the inevitable truth about aging.

"M&A takes a lot of time and energy," says DeVoe, "whether you are on one side or the other and your ability to be more focused, more structured, and to identify, you know, not this universe of frogs you need to kiss but just 'Aah, I'm only gonna kiss blue frogs that'—OK, that's a weird analogy now, but you know—you are more specific on the frogs you want to kiss. This can really save everyone time and energy."

Even when you meet the right blue frog, culture remains a critical part of the equation. DeVoe says, "The cultures need to 'mesh' as opposed to 'match'" in order for a transaction to be successful. The idea of meshing versus matching means that you need to get along and adapt as opposed to having an identical overlap of skills and style. DeVoe has an interesting take on when a seller wants an exact match:

Seeking an identical culture is perhaps an indicator that a seller isn't psychologically ready to sell. There needs to be a balance: strategic power or fit, business model alignment, economics, and culture are all paramount. Investment philosophy is an easy screen up front; cultural fit takes more time to evaluate."

This might seem obvious, but I can tell you from experience that countless advisors make the beginner's mistake of ignoring or minimizing the crucial aspect of cultural fit.

Some of the recent trends are focused on succession planning and, more recently, strategic planning. Moreover, DeVoe has also completed some projects with clients on the human capital side, known as "incentive compensation." Some clients come to him after building great businesses, and they can be overwhelmed by their choices at that level. For example, they can grow their core business faster, enter new markets, acquire other firms, or even sell and move on to other ventures. As firms grow, they bring on more associates and partners, which can be great for growth but a real drag when you have ten-person executive committee meetings. As these firms grow, they all want to incentivize and motivate their employees in the most efficient way possible. In other words, the issue becomes about how to mold, modify, and change behavior patterns.

A January 2019 article by Charles Paikert from the publication *Financial Planning* quotes DeVoe as saying, "Five years from now, I can see a dozen or so mega firms dominating the industry. For the first twelve to fourteen years that I tracked M&A, the key driver for sellers was exiting the business. Now the desire to achieve scale is the primary driver." Some other experts describe a similar vision of the future. Brent Brodeski, CEO of Savant Management in Illinois, says, "I think you'll see ten to fifteen large firms that will be dominant regionally and a few who may have a truly national presence. It's just the way the industry is developing." DeVoe and Brodeski are right on the mark. In March of 2019, it was announced that NFP, one of the original aggregators from fifteen years ago, agreed to acquire the $6 billion advisory firm Bronfman Rothschild. In an ironic twist, Bronfman had already established itself as an M&A acquirer prior to this transaction. The acquirer was acquired by a larger firm.

The trends that will continue to shape the M&A market are the aging of firm owners, financial pressure to improve scale and efficiency, and relatively high valuations due to the availability of money. For example, one statistic I heard in an interview was that there are more CFPs over the age of seventy than under the age of thirty. The industry will need to create new jobs to absorb the wave of retiring advisors, another unavoidable truth. Someday, these advisors must sell. Another oft cited number is that due to increased competition, management fees have generally come down over the past ten years. Moreover, private equity capital and bankers (like Live Oak Bank, which you will read about later) have started to focus their lending on the financial services industry. This ready supply of money has helped increase valuations and moved deals along at a faster pace.

The industry is often segmented into different tranches based on asset size:

- Smallest: Firms with less than $100 million in AUM

- Midsize: Firms from $100 million to $1 billion in AUM

- Largest (serial acquirers): Firms with over $1 billion in AUM

DeVoe continues, "There are over five thousand RIAs with over $100 million in AUM. There could easily be two to three times more of those firms coming to market than we're currently seeing. If that happens in a given year, supply could outstrip demand, and valuations could drop drastically." In my opinion, this is exactly why you want to play the long game and be prepared for when this event could happen. Start your plans now, modify them as necessary, and be patient. No one is getting any younger.

So one key takeaway is that these firms in the middle might get squeezed, and they should adjust their future plans to incorporate this possibility. Two areas these smaller firms (mine included) can focus on are acquisitions and technology enhancements. I have told my team on several occasions to get ready for "the wave" of sellers that might happen in any given year. In addition, I have asked them to continually look for areas where technology can leverage operations or client service and experience. For example, we use an application called VoiceShot a few times a year to remind clients of important seminars or conference calls, and this is all done with my recorded voice and the appropriate compliance disclosures. The truth is that all firms, big and small, have to get more efficient with their back-office operations and client service models.

There is some good news for solo firms in the opinion of these veterans. DeVoe says, "I don't see them being decimated like small travel agencies were. You can earn a very good living as a solo practitioner. That cohort is not going away." Another industry veteran, Michael Kitces of Pinnacle Advisory Group, feels the same way. He believes solo advisors who are CFPs will be fine, and the so-called industry mandate for smaller firms to grow and scale up may be overhyped.

I have seen this firsthand over the past fifteen years when I look back on the dozens and dozens of firms I have interacted with through my acquisition process. In martial arts, the most traditional styles tend to have staying power. That is, the instructors who intentionally stay with tradition and smaller classes and resist the need to become mega karate studios often have the most loyal, proficient, and well-respected students. The smaller firms tend to have loyal clients who stay with them for the long haul. Not every client and not every martial artist needs to be with a conglomerate.

Critical risks do remain for the smaller RIAs and IBD firms. A lingering bear market, a wave of aging baby-boomer owners selling at the same time, or a lethal combination of both could drastically drive down prices. DeVoe thinks there is a 30 percent chance of that happening in the next seven years or so. With the recent stock market volatility and the swift and severe correction in December 2018, the M&A market has seen quite a lot of volatility. Another top executive from Mercer Advisors, Dave Barton, puts it this way: "I think sellers are still guided by 2018 and believe they can get top dollar. They're going to have to clean up their profit and loss lines and understand that buyers are buying risk, and the risk is increasing."

The truth is advisors are all getting older. Valuations are stretched, and there is not a lot of upside on multiples right now. M&A planning takes time, emotional energy, and a disciplined approach. Advisors need to get educated thoroughly and quickly or they will miss out on the greatest transition in history. Don't be left behind.

The truth is hidden in plain sight. Time is not on your side if you are procrastinating. Make time your ally by creating a strategy for the long haul.

KEY ACTION STEPS/TAKEAWAYS

1. Acquisitions are a major part of financial services today. You should read about them, study them, and get to know what makes them work. Someday when it comes time to sell or merge your firm, you will be more knowledgeable about valuation and succession planning.

2. Acknowledge the challenges that come with setting up a succession plan, especially if you are a solo advisor or with a smaller wealth management firm.

3. Assets under management (AUM) are the lifeblood of most advisory firms. Know where your firm stands in terms of the hierarchy in this industry. Have an action plan based on the size, scope, and direction of your firm.

CHAPTER 5

THE FIVE ELEMENTS OF POWER

———

"If you're fully prepared, you need not worry."

—JAPANESE PROVERB

As I look out over the landscape of the M&A market, it becomes abundantly clear to me that anyone who wants to succeed in this space must be organized, efficient, and prepared. Beyond the obvious reasons to be organized (less stress, more clarity, more fun) lies a more capitalist reason: money. You need to know the players, strategies, and techniques in order to save money if you are a buyer or maximize money if you are a seller.

If you work with both buyers and sellers, you must have a keen grasp of the needs of these distinct yet interconnected landscapes. Buyers and sellers are often like giant financial tectonic plates, constantly brushing up against one another, causing a rippling effect in the industry each time contact is made. I can think of no one better to guide us through this M&A lithosphere than Dan Kreuter.

Dan Kreuter is chairman at Gladstone Group, an M&A advisory firm that provides many different services for the independent financial advisory sector across the United States. Gladstone can provide buy side, sell side, merger advisory, and corporate planning for firms that range from $3 million to $50 million in revenue. Long before he started Gladstone Associates LLC in 2006, he was honing his craft of being prepared and a step ahead of the competition.

THE BEGINNING OF DAK

Dan Kreuter started a headhunting/recruiting business in 1979 called D. A. Kreuter & Associates (DAK). This era was the end of the Glass–Steagall era of regulation, and everyone was getting into everyone else's businesses. For example, banks were selling insurance products and securities, and insurance companies started their own broker-dealers and were selling bank products along with stocks and bonds. As Dan eloquently puts it, "DAK Associates was like the tour guide in Europe that spoke French, English, German, and a little bit of Greek." Dan was able to build a sustainable, growing, retainer-based executive search firm in the areas of asset management, wealth management, insurance, and retirement services.

Over the years as DAK grew, he took the intellectual property he was creating and brought it over to the investment banking and M&A advisory business landscape. *Dan adds, "M&A is really headhunting on steroids. Instead of moving people, you move entire companies, and you have to be handy with spreadsheets, org charts, legal and compliance issues. You have to be a jack of all trades."* You have to be prepared. This is similar to martial arts in that you have to learn many techniques to get better over time, even if eventually you continue to perfect a certain punch or kick. In the first four to six years of training, when you typically get your black belt (*shodan*), these basic techniques provide the foundation for the rest of your martial arts training.

Gladstone has created a playbook of every aggregator in the country. He knows the competition very well. A very famous quote from the Japanese warrior Miyamoto Musashi says, "Know your enemy, know his sword." Dan certainly knows the sword of the competition. Some of the proprietary data is from their clients, which is always kept secret, and other parts of this playbook are from internal research. One big advantage in using Gladstone is their flexibility. Selling a firm isn't always the answer. As Dan says, "Why sell the golden goose?" The term he uses for a completed succession plan is "papered and funded." This means an advisor has done all the correct legal paperwork and has a funding mechanism (usually life insurance) that will provide capital to the firm if and when the owner should die or retire. His philosophy is that if the advisor has created a solid brand, has great staffing, good profit margins, and a smart business plan, maybe selling is not the best idea. His executive search firm might be able to bring in a good CEO or COO to help run the business while the owner stays involved but takes time away to travel and enjoy life. Everybody wins.

Who are the acquirers out there in the marketplace today? Dan breaks down the players into four distinct groups.

The first group is what he calls the big national platform companies that have an RIA and advisory platform. This group is typically backed by private equity (some have their own balance sheets), and these firms are looking to acquire year-round. They could be called "serial acquirers."

The next group is large RIAs, typically from $2 billion to $4 billion in size, that want to get bigger or perhaps open an office in San Francisco or New York. These two groups represent about 75 percent of the buyers today.

Banks represent the third major category. These banks are usually looking to diversify their asset base and revenue stream, so they may only make one or two large acquisitions and that will be sufficient for their needs. Basically, they want to get more market share or wallet share in their geographical footprint.

The rest of the acquirers, the fourth group Dan calls "everyone else," could include large property and casualty or benefits firms and the CPA firms looking to add advisory services. These entities already have the clients who need the wealth management advice, so there is a reverse-engineering approach to this problem. These acquirers are gaining employees like CFPs who can give the advice along with the actual entity—the advisory firm—that generates the revenue.

One more group rarely gets public attention. This group would include firms like my own, Capital Wealth Management, and smaller firms under $250 million of AUM. What is interesting is that many if not all of these smaller deals don't get reported in the press and therefore go under the radar. If you add in the large broker-dealers like LPL and Cambridge, many if not all of their transactions between their advisors do not go reported, and the assets are thus kept "in-house." This is a strategic advantage for these firms because they keep the data—such as price, deal structure, and terms—private.

So what should you expect from doing a deal in today's market? What are the benefits to being in this M&A mania? Dan wants his clients to focus on Five Elements of Power that should accrue to both buyer and seller in any M&A transaction, but we will focus on these aspects from the seller's perspective below. As always, you must be fully prepared when you enter this marketplace.

THE FIVE ELEMENTS OF POWER

1. Buying Power

2. Solutions and Services Power

3. Brand Power

4. Staying Power

5. People Power

Buying power. The larger the firm you build, the more leverage you have with product providers, custodians (where the client's money is actually held), and technology services. When you sell to a larger firm, these benefits accrue to your firm.

Solutions and services power allows one firm to sell to another firm that has strengths in areas you don't. For instance, the firm you sell to might have strengths in charitable giving, the 401(k) market, and perhaps advanced estate planning. Your clients benefit from access to and the solutions of these additional services.

Brand power can be an advantage if you sell to the right firm that has already created a regional or national brand with strong social media support, client-centered events, and ongoing touch points throughout the year.

Staying power is one of the strongest reasons to consider selling, because you get to advertise to your clients that the next generation of the firm, or G2 as it is called, has already been established. My personal experience is that you or your firm gathers more assets and gets the children and grandchildren involved as clients when this process is executed correctly. Now the clients don't worry (as much) about what happens if the owner gets hit by the proverbial beer truck (I would prefer the Stella Artois truck if I had the choice). Moreover, the founder or owner can stay on to mentor the G2 owners and share wisdom and knowledge.

People power is the last item but is of no less importance than the others. When you sell to a larger platform that is well-run and efficient, your team and clients can tap into an even larger team with certain specialties and strengths. One transaction that I was recently involved with allowed my firm to systematize and explain the investment process far better than the original advisor was able to do. She was more than happy to brag to her clients that she wanted them to see our investment methodology and all the new team members that could support her and her client base. These personnel strengths are often difficult to acquire, regardless if you try to develop in-house or recruit on the open market.

Before you enter the M&A market, whether as a buyer or seller, you really have to be prepared. You have to have your ducks in a row. Over the years, Dan has seen many cases of operating agreements that are antiquated, not well written, or not even in place. In addition, people think they have succession plans but they are not "papered and funded, so they are not really succession plans at all." This is analogous to the personal side of the planning business that I have witnessed. My team and I have seen many cases of wills not being signed, references to trust agreements that don't exist, and beneficiary forms that are blank or incorrectly filled out. During my many years of training in martial arts, my instructor would often comment, very vocally, if he saw a student with their karate *gi* (ghee), or uniform, out of place. If your belt was tied wrong, or your uniform was dirty, this was considered very unprepared. He would ask rhetorically, "How can you go to battle when your uniform is dirty and you are unprepared?"

Corporate planning is not a strength of some asset gatherers and wealth advisors, though clearly it is a vital skill set that needs to be filled. Dan says, "They are good at finding and running money, learning new products and comprehensive financial planning, but not closely held corporate planning. They have good businesses with good margins; however, they are not necessarily businesses that professional buyers are attracted to."

What does the future hold for the M&A business? Dan predicts that more multibillion-dollar RIAs will merge with each other, the same way banks have done over the last twenty years. Dan just heard of a private transaction where two large RIAs of equal value merged, and neither knew the other one was for sale. He foresees a lot more $5 billion to $10 billion AUM/RIA mergers with national or coastal footprints altering the M&A landscape as well. These combined firms will have a lot of purchasing power, brand power, people power, and pricing power. These new multibillion-dollar RIA behemoths will make it very tough for the small or midsize firms to compete.

Dan has another theory about the future of this RIA feeding frenzy. "My crystal ball tells me I wouldn't be surprised to see even the national aggregators join up together. Why wouldn't they continue to improve on brand, people, pricing, and purchasing power?"

What type of firms might prosper in this new financial environment? Dan sees a very clear path to success, even if you are not the eight-hundred-pound gorilla of the neighborhood.

You can definitely stay alive and thrive as a $2 million to $3 million revenue boutique where the founder/owner has a trusted number two person and a team of CFPs or CFAs doing the analysis. People like working with a boutique approach. Fine French restaurants can't be franchised. Not everything has to be franchised or scaled.

According to several industry experts, to reiterate, over 70 percent of the investment firms are below $100 million in AUM. Here is the challenge moving forward. From a pricing perspective, the larger firms will have a lot of pricing power with technology vendors, custodians, service providers, and money managers. The logic then flows that if a current or potential client of a smaller boutique firm pays 1 percent a year in management fees, and if they can get nearly the same thing from a larger firm for twenty basis points or one fifth of what they are now paying, Dan says, "People will vote with their feet and move the accounts." The answer? You must focus on your target market and not try to be all things to all people.

You can't be going in two directions at once; that is, trying to get bigger without the proper infrastructure or staying small and losing the technology battle. My advice on this area is to focus on a plan and continue to improve it. As market conditions change, you must be prepared. If you are prepared, then you can change. If you change and adapt, you don't have to worry.

KEY ACTION STEPS/TAKEAWAYS

1. Be consciously aware of the Five Elements of Power if you are involved in any type of transaction.

2. Be prepared as you enter this market. Some firms are great asset gatherers but not so good at corporate planning.

3. Be price sensitive. Watch how the larger firms are compressing fees through the use of technology.

CHAPTER 6

ECHELON PARTNERS

——

"The expectations of life depend upon diligence; the mechanic that would perfect his work must first sharpen his tools."

—CONFUCIUS

When we talk about the M&A business or succession and continuity planning, it is critical to know exactly what we are talking about. Just as math is precise, we need to make sure we are all talking about the same thing. We need to understand the trends, categories, and where your firm fits into those categories. And we must collectively sharpen our tools in order to take advantage of these trends.

I am always amazed when I attend conferences or read white papers at how much the average advisor doesn't know or doesn't care about our industry. Much of that comes from either lack of knowledge or simply preserving the status quo. Either way, that is a dangerous way to conduct business if you want to maximize your profit when you sell or enjoy your lengthy career as you build your business.

Therefore, in order to educate you about some of the trends, we need to understand the categories of this industry and how we fit into them. How do we grow efficiently, with purpose, if we don't know where we are in the world of M&A? We need to know about the key components of M&A, what drives valuation, and how firms like ECHELON Partners segment and classify this profitable industry.

One person who has a great grasp of the M&A landscape is Carolyn Armitage.

CAROLYN'S CAREER

Carolyn has spent years sharpening her mental intellect, from a childhood bet with her brother regarding math lessons to a challenging corporate career with all of its natural twists and turns.

Carolyn Armitage, managing director for ECHELON Partners, has a warm and inviting smile. She is thoughtful, articulate, and organized. She has decades of experience in the

IBD and RIA marketplace. She attributes her appreciation of math and the numbers aspect of the financial services business to one of her older brothers. When she was in second grade, Carolyn's brother proposed to teach her how to multiply and divide (something she normally wouldn't have learned until third and fourth grade) if she would clean his room. While Carolyn didn't fancy cleaning, she loved the prospect of learning something new and always enjoys a worthy challenge. The bet was made, and ever since then, Carolyn has taken on and overcome many challenges in the financial services industry.

Carolyn's career took her from Minneapolis to Dallas and finally Los Angeles. In Dallas, she worked at a small start-up CPA firm and eventually helped them during their IPO. She arrived in Los Angeles just in time to help foster the fee-based asset management practice at a corporate RIA. When the financial crisis hit in 2008, she had to make some changes again by joining a major broker-dealer and consulting for large "Super OSJs."

For those not familiar with this term, OSJ stands for Office of Supervisory Jurisdiction, and at its core, it's basically a branch manager for many financial advisors. I am an OSJ for my firm, but these "Super OSJs" are on a scale of five to ten times the size of my firm. There are many challenges in running a complex "Super OSJ" such as compliance, technology, and licensing. This was a terrific opportunity for Carolyn to apply all her years of experience in a consulting capacity, which would prove essential for her role at ECHELON Partners.

ECHELON OVERVIEW

ECHELON has a unique network of strategic partners, some nonfinancial, that provide additional resources as needed for their investment banking activities. For example, there are ten disciplines listed on their website, such as national accounting and law firms, private equity and venture capital investors, and turnkey asset management platforms. This high-quality network gives them the ability to conduct valuable research, make powerful introductions, and achieve greater success for their clients.

In addition, Carolyn says, *At ECHELON, we pride ourselves on providing a holistic approach to the wealth and investment management industries by offering investment banking (through ECHELON Capital Partners), management consulting, and valuation services. We can help clients through the entire life cycle of their business from entity formation through transitioning and sunsetting their careers.*" The approximate breakdown of their business is 40 percent investment banking, 30 percent management consulting, and 30 percent valuation.

ECHELON understands the wealth management market-place so well that they shared three categories for us to better identify where we each fit. Carolyn describes the three categories as "practices or books of business, followed by boutiques and then small businesses." The *books of business* category includes firms with less than $200 million in AUM, *boutique* firms have $200 million to $1 billion in AUM, and firms over $1 billion in AUM are considered *businesses*. Carolyn and her partners serve the latter two categories, those firms with $200 million to several billion in AUM.

From her current perch at ECHELON Partners, Carolyn summarizes these six key components of the marketplace in order for the reader to better understand the M&A landscape:

- Growth

- Scale

- Environment for mergers and acquisitions (M&A)

- Sellers mind-set

- Buyers mind-set

- Valuation (on a case-by-case basis)

The main drivers of firm valuation are the first and second categories, growth and scale.

Whether it is a practice, a boutique, or a business, growth is what buyers are seeking. Growth can come in many forms—revenue, assets, number of clients, expenses and profit, or profit margin. Along with growth rates over the past five years, she looks at scale of the organization and the ability to add more clients and assets with low or no additional expenses. Growth and scale are two of the largest drivers impacting valuations. To get a sense of the scope of the business we are dealing with, Carolyn shared a chart of RIA firms by total number and by total assets.

RIA—Total Number of Firms

RIA—Number of Firms:

- Under $100 million of AUM: 75 percent.

- From $100 million to $500 million of AUM: 18.5 percent.

- From $500 million to $1 billion of AUM: 3.5 percent.

- Over $1 billion of AUM: 3 percent.

Now for the assets of those firms:

- At least $1 billion or more of AUM: 56.5 percent.

- From $200 million to $1 billion of AUM: 25.5 percent.

- Under $200 million of AUM: 18 percent.

The M&A landscape is a robust environment due to several factors. Demographics, interest rates, and available capital all have economic tailwinds at this time.

Carolyn is ebullient when she says, "The stock market is doing fairly well, interest rates are low, there is lots of liquidity, profit margins have never been better, and the IPO market is very small." Why would the IPO market have any bearing on this? "With fewer opportunities in the IPO marketplace, the private equity money is looking for a place to invest. Private equity looks for the best alternatives for the return on their capital, and wealth management is the most profitable segment in financial services." Wealth management businesses are so desirable that money is readily available from banks and private equity firms to help with exit strategies and buyouts. Moreover, the average age of the owners and advisors is well above sixty, producing a perfect storm for merger and exit mania.

The sellers' and buyers' mind-sets are so unique that each situation needs to be viewed on a case-by-case basis. Because of the ready supply of buyers, ECHELON has an intentional investment banking process to ensure the proper fit of personality, business acumen, and investment philosophy. They provide the buyers and sellers ample opportunities to get to know each other and observe consistent behavior. For example, if a seller is pushing too fast to close a deal, that will naturally lead to speculation that there is some sort of "distress sale" going on and can affect valuation.

Sellers have a very difficult decision to make when they decide to place their firm up for sale. Often sellers struggle with an "inner dialogue" about the pros and cons of selling their firm. For example, sellers often handpick their clients and know them extremely well. As CEOs of their own firm, they have a sense of command and control on a day-to-day basis. But that all changes when they sell their business. What is their new role in the firm, in society, and at home with their spouse? They lose command and control, and the owner may feel a loss of sense or purpose. Carolyn says, "These decisions are gut-wrenching and very emotional."

The buyer's mind-set depends on their knowledge and experience. In today's marketplace, many buyers are not prepared for an acquisition and will often fumble through and struggle for their first acquisition. This is just like getting your first million-dollar client—you need to learn, rehearse, and review often. I am sure we all remember (as I clearly do) the times in our career that we were not prepared for or familiar with a new situation or a new type of client, and that lack of preparation clearly showed. Those were the times in our career that we were not "perfecting our work" because we did not "sharpen our tools."

You must think of acquisitions as a white belt would, as a beginner would, where many possibilities exist. Practice and preparation are key, just like learning kata (forms) or *kumite* (sparring). Recall I mentioned earlier that even when I was an advanced black belt, my instructor, Sensei Mori, had me work for *one whole year* to improve just one punch, yet I had been doing this punch for over a decade already!

WHEN IS THE SELLER READY TO SELL?

The ability to identify if an advisor is ready to sell is another key component in your due diligence tool belt. An advisor's financial and mental readiness to leave their business are two important components that are sometimes overlooked.

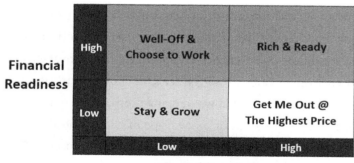

		Low	High
Financial Readiness	**High**	Well-Off & Choose to Work	Rich & Ready
	Low	Stay & Grow	Get Me Out @ The Highest Price

Mental Readiness

Some advisors, the *Well-Off & Choose to Work*, have the financial means to retire but cannot envision themselves not working, so they put off selling for as long as they are able, which often results in their client base aging and stagnating, causing their practice to eventually lose its value. These advisors can be the most frustrating type of acquisition candidate, because they will go to the one-yard line with you and then punt indefinitely.

Other advisors are *Rich & Ready* and have both the financial means to move on from their business and the desire to sell and are the most ideal but hardest type of acquisition candidate to find.

Stay & Grow advisors do not yet have the financial readiness nor desire to sell. This group may include younger advisors or those just starting in their career and probably can be quickly eliminated as potential acquisitions.

Finally, *Get Me Out at the Highest Price* advisors are those who may not be financially ready to retire but, due to outside circumstances, want to leave their practice. Sometimes this is due to health or personal reasons, other times it has to do with disillusionment with the realities of running a practice. These types of advisors often become more motivated to sell during times of extreme market volatility.

Many practice owners seek a "back of the napkin" or DIY (do it yourself) approach to valuation due to its simplicity and cost—free! However, it often leads to erroneous conclusions. For example, determining a valuation based on a multiple of revenue (or GDC revenue in the IBD world) doesn't include the cost of doing business.

For *boutiques* and *businesses*, the preferred approach is to use a multiple of earnings before interest, tax, depreciation, and amortization (EBITDA). Valuations of IBD firms versus RIA firms are different, as the quality of their revenue streams are different, the nature of their businesses are different, and their advisors are often affiliated differently, which can have implications of the degree of risk in a deal. This approach really focuses on the overall profitability or "health" of the entity, not just the revenues.

It's like focusing your own health and diet regimen on one number, BMI (Body Mass Index), and not looking at other key health metrics like blood pressure, cholesterol, blood sugar, and genetics. In this analogy, the BMI is like a multiple of revenue approach, whereas the other health metrics like blood pressure and cholesterol are more akin to a valuation based on a multiple of EBITDA.

Another reason firms may want or need a more comprehensive EBITDA approach is that a lender may not loan money based on a multiple of revenue (GDC). Often, they prefer other methods that consider the expenses. When an advisor has multiple revenue streams, each needs to be valued and linked to the overall firm value.

When you are looking to sell your business, sometimes, the more moving parts your firm has, the more difficult it is to find another buyer who has or wants all those matching parts. Therefore, a firm within the IBD channel is more likely to sell to another firm in the IBD channel, even within their own broker-dealer, as there is "less risk of breakage" according to Carolyn. However, if the IBD channel is shrinking and the RIA channel is growing rapidly, how might that affect your future business plans?

The RIA model is a streamlined wealth management business model. A single, fee-only revenue stream and centralized (or outsourced) asset management and processes often make for tighter operations and compliance, and an employed advisor base makes the RIA firm model much more desirable than the older 1099 independent contractor business model.

Moreover, larger RIA firms are able to offer more services and options where they custody client assets, such as multiple clearing firms like Schwab, Fidelity, and Pershing. With more clearing firms (custodians) and a streamlined business model, you have the ability to serve a larger audience. RIA firms often sell for a higher multiple than a similar size IBD firm due to the consistency (predictability) of revenue and other risk-mitigating factors.

One other major consideration to be aware of is each firm can have multiple valuations. A valuation only makes sense in context. For example, a firm for sale will be worth more to one buyer than another; therefore, some will be willing to pay more than others. What if your firm is an exact fit for a buyer who wants to expand into your geographical area? What if your products and services are exactly the areas the buyer wants to grow and expand into? In these cases, your value to this buyer is more than it is to others.

With increasing interest from experienced private equity firms and an active dealmaking environment, you may want to proceed with caution and consider using credible experts to guide you through this process—just as you guide your clients into and through retirement, investment bankers are your "retirement advisors."

Carolyn provides some clarity regarding the terms *M&A* versus *investment banking*. *M&A* has become the new "recruiting" or business development term in the industry, and dozens of M&A consultants are eager to help you for a fee. However, in order to transact a deal, one needs to be a licensed investment banker and use a broker-dealer to clear the transaction through.

Just as Carolyn sharpened her mental tools before and during her time at ECHELON Partners, we too must work hard to sharpen our tools, educate ourselves, and retain credible experts to guide us through this new paradigm.

After all, most of us will only get one chance to sell or merge our firm, and we want to get it right. We need to find the right "mechanic" that wants to perfect his work.

KEY ACTION STEPS/TAKEAWAYS

1. Know where you (and your firm) fit into this M&A landscape: a practice, a boutique, or a business.

2. Know the psychology of the seller (if you are a buyer) and vice versa. This will save you time and aggravation down the road.

3. Know that valuation only has meaning in context. The valuation will change over time, and that is not the number you sell for.

PART 3

FINANCING

CHAPTER 7

LIVE OAK BANK

———

"Nobody is superior, nobody is inferior, but nobody is equal either. People are simply unique, incomparable.""

−OSHO

I want to talk to you about the importance of being unique, especially in banking. It is important for a bank to be unique, especially as their client (customer) base grows and the needs of those clients expand and multiply. That's why I wanted to introduce you to Live Oak Bank. They are an outstanding example of a modern bank that truly understands what it means to be incomparable.

There is a lot of competition in banking today, especially as it relates to financial services for advisors. It is critical to be unique and innovative in order to gain market share and attract the right type of clients or customers. In most technology industries, including financial services, so many techniques and strategies are copied from one organization to the next at such a blinding pace that it can be difficult in the mind of the consumer (or the advisor) to differentiate between what is new and cutting-edge versus what is recycled glitz and glamor.

On their website, Live Oak Bank has a great mission statement that hints of their unusual approach to banking:

> Our mission is to create an unprecedented banking experience for small business owners nationwide, through service and technology. Live Oak Bank is not your traditional bank. With a laser focus on innovation in finance and technology, we bring efficiency and excellence to the lending process. We believe deeply in personal service and focus on taking care of our customers throughout the life of the relationship.

WHY ARE THEY UNIQUE?

James Hughes, VP of investment advisory lending at Live Oak Bank, explained why Live Oak is creative and unique. Live Oak Bank started in 2008, and they are located in

Wilmington, North Carolina. James tells the story of how the founder, James S. (Chip) Mahan III started the bank with several other partners in a garage as they worked on the bank charter in 2007. Their original focus was small-business lending, and the first industry they focused on was veterinarians. They were so well prepared that they hired two veterinarians on staff to help in the analysis and underwriting.

Their philosophy reminded me of the beginner's mind concept I shared with you in the introduction: the beginner sees many possibilities while the expert only sees a few.

What makes Live Oak Bank unique is that they're a cash flow lender. Banks traditionally use a loan-to-value ratio when approving deals, but Live Oak doesn't have that restriction. Because they focus on the advisory business, RIAs, and other wealth management firms, the balance sheets of these clients are very different from a typical client. As Hughes says, the "financial advisory business does not have any tangible collateral, they have the client list, the relationships, and a few laptops."

So what did they do? They created another niche lending group and started to learn about financial advisors the same way they learned about veterinarians. Boy, was their timing spot-on. The average age of the financial advisor industry is pushing sixty. Every expert I spoke to estimates that only 20–25 percent of practices have written succession plans, but even some of those are not funded properly if they lack a life insurance buy-and-sell arrangement. They are not "papered and funded," in the words of Dan Kreuter, CEO of Gladstone Group.

The second area in which they are unique is the compensation structure of their loan officers. Most banks employ commission-based loan officers who have an incentive to create bigger loans to grow their compensation. They employ a consultative approach to lending, and at Live Oak, these employees have equity stakes in the business. This structure creates a win-win scenario: the loan officer wants to offer quality loans to the right clients just as the RIAs or financial advisors wants to build their own book of business with the right clientele.

In martial arts, instructors often teach their students all the basic techniques in exactly the same way. But as you grow with your knowledge and technique, it was understood that you would develop your own unique combination of techniques, especially in *kumite* (sparring). For example, at the national and international tournaments, a good team captain or instructor would "scout" the opponents by watching them in the earlier matches. Eventually, your unique combination of techniques would be your signature, if you will, your unique style that could not be exactly copied. And it might just get you to the final round of competition.

The management team hired an executive out of Charles Schwab, another one out of Ameriprise, a former financial advisor, and even a CPA. They left no stone (or tree, ha ha) unturned! James spent ten years at Morgan Stanley and has his Series 7, which is the basic exam that advisors pass to obtain a license to solicit securities business and build a client base. Hughes joined the bank in October 2013. At Live Oak, they want a long-term banking relationship with the investment advisor community in several different areas. For example, if you need money for working capital, partner buy-ins, or even staged succession, they want to be your bank of choice. Their target market is advisors with assets of $50 million to $250 million, and their average loan amount, the principal, is in the neighborhood of $1 million.

While there were other lenders in the marketplace prior to Live Oak, Live Oak really focused on this market aggressively and on a nationwide basis. Live Oak was playing the long game, building up resources and contacts and capabilities. They consciously formed relationships with broker-dealers, custodians, and valuation companies, all in the financial services field. Hughes adds, *"Live Oak really educated the investment industry that there was bank financing available on a mass scale. Since that time, a few lenders have come out of the woodwork as well."* They also shifted the thinking of the industry in a dramatic way. They educated advisors that growing your business inorganically through acquisitions was a smart way to grow.

Advisors are now more educated about the acquisition market, how deals are done, and that deals can get done. This has driven more interest in the financing aspect of the business.

The old way a deal was structured before 2013 was 10 percent down and the rest paid out over three to five years from the earnings of that business. The majority of the risk was with the seller, who had to make sure the client relationships were securely transferred to the new advisor and those clients had to stay for three to five years with the new buyer in order for the deal to work out. If the stock market went south in that "earn out" period, the deal would take even longer to break even. These were the dark ages, if you will, of the M&A and succession-planning industry.

Now Live Oak is doing deals that are "positive cash flow from day one" according to Hughes. That means they finance the whole purchase price up front, and the buyer has ten years to pay off the loan. Contrast that with the old way of doing business, and you quickly see the reason why this niche has grown so fast. The old way involved a 10 percent down payment, but it took three to five years to pay off the loan and make the deal work.

Regarding my own personal situation, my first transaction was completed in September 2004 under this old scenario of the three-to-five-year earn out. After taxes and the earn-out payment, I would have lost money but for the fact that I doubled the assets of that firm by getting great referrals.

The tax angle is critically important here. If the seller can get more of the money up front, they can get capital gains treatment on that money while the buyer has to treat that money as earned income or "ordinary income." The industry has become so competitive that the sellers are dictating terms, and as the sellers continue to meet and spread the word, the down payments have gone from 10 percent in the old days to 40 to 50 percent now and sometimes higher. In some cases, with a good economy and multiple buyers, they can get an all-cash deal and walk away with no risk.

VALUATION AND THE W2 MODEL

Many people in our industry are curious about valuation differences between RIA and IBD firms. James Hughes thinks that if revenue and EBITDA are the same, regardless of the type of firm, the valuation should be the same. However, he does add that once you get over $1 billion in assets and you have a sustainable practice with enterprise value, those valuations or multiples would increase. Most IBD (broker-dealer) firms don't get over $500 million in assets, and those that do tend to shift over to the RIA model. Therefore, once a firm gets large enough in assets, they almost always shift to the RIA model. Hughes says it is not uncommon to see RIA firms grow to $5 billion, $10 billion, or $20 billion in assets.

A traditional EBITDA multiple might be three to five times for smaller firms (under $250 million), but it is not uncommon to see those numbers go from seven to ten times EBITDA with the larger firms whose assets exceed $1 billion. It clearly makes sense with this increased valuation why so many firms want to be serial acquirers or merge with larger firms, as this enhances value and allows more opportunity for growth.

An important point Hughes made around valuation was the creation of "enterprise" value. In order to create value for your firm, you need to adopt a W2 model versus a 1099 model. The 1099 model often allows the producing advisors to be independent of the firm and therefore take the client assets with them if they leave. In addition, the 1099 model allows for the producing advisors to take higher compensation through their payout, which limits the bottom line of the firm. By having your producing advisors as W2 employees, the firm owns the client assets, and in turn, the firm holds the value of the client assets. Typically, the advisors are paid a wage and then eventually will own equity and participate in distributions from the business. This model incentivizes advisors and owners to work toward a similar goal, grow the client base, and grow the bottom line. The current thinking is that the W2 model is superior. A "one for all and all for one" approach.

The 1099 model has a splinter effect in that those advisors technically have some "ownership" of those clients, so when it comes time for an advisor to sell, you have a challenge. The challenge is that the revenue generated in the 1099 model, the independent contractor status, could be considered revenue for the advisor individually but not of the firm, so those assets would not count as part of AUM when a firm is up for sale. The W2 model caps out on the salary, but then you offer equity to the employee, whereas in the 1099 model, you just keep growing the assets by taking on more clients without any overall thought to the big picture. Again, this industry is gravitating toward the W2 model because the advisor and the firm have aligned interests. For many years, the 1099 model was the standard, but now the industry has properly shifted to the W2 model.

Everyone thinks that this flood of deals will happen each year because of the demographics and the great stock market. It is ironic that with a good stock market and stable economy, there *aren't* a flood of deals coming to market. My thoughts on this parallel those of James Hughes: advisors tend to stick around and run the asset base to zero over time. The truth is, once clients get to trust an advisor, they tend to stay around for a long time, and attrition rates are low in this industry. If you are playing the long game, you want to start your transition years before your end date. That will allow you the best chance of success while still growing your client base.

However, all the experts I spoke to also said that the advisor who stays too long and does not continually improve the practice creates an environment of diminishing returns. Each year, that practice tends to lose clients to death, physical relocation, and competition. Sadly, some advisors don't really care about this. Even worse, many advisors die without clear succession or continuity plans, leaving clients in the lurch. In my fifteen years of acquisitions, I have personally witnessed three occasions where the advisors died while delaying negotiations with my firm only to have their spouses receive little or no value for a lifetime's worth of work. Shockingly incomprehensible.

AVERAGE DEAL STRUCTURE

The average deal structure is now 50–75 percent up-front payment with the remaining money going into an escrow account, or the back end can be financed by a promissory note with the seller. Also, the tax allocation clause, according to other experts, is currently 83 percent goodwill, 13 percent consulting agreement (for transition assistance), and 4 percent allocated toward a noncompete agreement. Hughes also stated that their average loan is right at $1 million. The buyer should always have clawbacks or clauses in the contract that protect him from clients leaving. Live Oak typically only deals with the buyers because those are the people that seek them out. They don't do any matching of buyers and sellers, nor do they promise to find a seller if they have an interested buyer seek them out.

The two top reasons why Hughes says some deals don't work out are (1) a weak relationship or lack of precise communication with the seller and (2) the seller staying on too long and having continued contact with his former clients.

Hughes says, "You should be very wary when the seller will have continued meaningful contact with the clients after the transition period has ended." The reason this becomes an issue is the clients get a mixed message; they don't know whom to contact for their stock market questions and service issues. Do they call the new advisor (the buyer) for advice or service, or do they call their former advisor (the seller) for those same concerns? As you will see later on, there can be disastrous consequences if the seller has continued contact with clients.

The typical transition takes anywhere from three to six months. I suggested to Hughes, and he agreed, that the way around this risk is some simple legal language in the purchase and sale agreement. For example, if the advisor is selling both a tax practice and an investment practice, you might have a clause that limits the seller's interaction with clients after the first tax season has finished.

Hughes also said they have added a real simple clause called "a do not disparage clause" that says you can't talk badly about the buyer or seller in case of any disputes. Another document that is important to have for your employees is a noncompete and a non-solicitation agreement; they can be wrapped into one document. This prevents unhappy employees or advisors from leaving and contacting the clients on their own, which would clearly create chaos in your retirement plan if you are in the middle of selling to a new advisor or a new firm.

UNDERSTANDING TODAY'S FINANCING LANDSCAPE

In today's world, independent financial advisors have a lot of options when it comes to financing. Different types of lending institutions offer financing to our industry. There is the traditional bank, like Live Oak Bank, and then there is the world of loan brokers, which comprises the majority of the other options in the market today. Both options have their benefits. I talked with James Hughes from Live Oak Bank about the two most common types of loans made to advisors, SBA loans and conventional loans. Live Oak Bank provides both.

Hughes talked about the two products they offer at Live Oak Bank as a full solution. Depending on the need of their customer, they can offer either product. Conventional and SBA loans have their advantages and disadvantages, so understanding that is key in seeking financing. From Hughes's perspective, conventional loans are more difficult to qualify for, those loans are on a shorter term (five to seven years), have lower advance rates, require stronger borrowers, require stronger cash flow, and often include loan covenants like prepayment penalties, minimum debt service coverage ratios, and holding a minimum cash balance in the checking account at the bank.

An SBA loan has a government guarantee (typically 75 percent guaranteed), so it is less risky for the bank. SBA lending has traditionally had lower underwriting requirements than conventional lending programs. The SBA program was really put in place for businesses that could not get conventional financing. The SBA loans are on a longer term (ten years), have higher advance rates, and do not include loan covenants. To clarify, the advance rate is how much of the deal can be financed. To get an understanding of what the bank is looking at, the difference in risk to the bank is this: if the conventional loan of $1 million goes south, there is no business collateral to collect, and if the advisor doesn't have enough personal assets, the bank essentially loses the whole value of the loan. The SBA loan is a different story with a better ending. For that same $1 million loan, in a worst-case scenario, 75 percent or $750,000 of that loan is guaranteed by the government. I wish my investment accounts had that level of downside protection!

Hughes walked me through the current rate structure for loans. There are many factors to consider when picking a rate. Live Oak offers a variety of rate options. Fixed rates, just like a fixed mortgage rate, are the easiest to understand. If you take a fixed rate for the life of the loan, then there is no risk of rising rates. The variable rate loans adjust throughout the life of the loan, typically quarterly, so the interest rate might increase or the decrease. You can also get a hybrid, or mixture, of a fixed and variable. This would be a rate that is fixed for a period of time and then changes to variable. I find it interesting that, according to Hughes, the variable rate is the most popular choice now. If I were borrowing money for ten years to buy a practice, I would want to lock in my expenses, at a reasonable rate of course, and not have to worry about future rate changes.

"We provide investment advisory financing solutions to help you position your firm for success now and into the future. You might think the lowest interest rate is what you should look for in a loan, but a low rate doesn't always mean the best funding option for your investment advisory firm."

When we think of all the unique things Live Oak does, from a unique charter that allows for cash flow lending, a smart compensation structure for their loan officers, laser focus on the customer experience, and some online resources that allow for preapproval, you might wonder if they are publicly traded yet. Yes, they are. In 2015, they went public under the symbol LOB.

Live Oak is in a class by themselves at the moment. Nobody is equal to them yet. Live Oak Bank set the standard by using traditional banking products in a modern way, which hearkens back to their innovative roots in cash flow lending and keen focus on the unique needs of the small business owner.

But intense competition is already around the corner, maybe not superior yet, not inferior, not equal. Just different.

KEY ACTION STEPS/TAKEAWAYS

1. Focus your actions and strategy to become known for something unique, preferably something hard to imitate or copy.

2. Financing is critical. You need to know the fine details of bank financing options and how they integrate with terms and deal structure.

3. Fine-tune your acquisition or succession strategy by talking to banks that specialize in working with financial advisors.

PART 4

BROKER-DEALER

CHAPTER 8

BRETT—CEO OF A REGIONAL BROKER-DEALER

"In the midst of chaos, there is also opportunity."

—SUN TZU

FINDING THE *KYO*

I believe in the world of M&A it is vital to know what the competition is doing and how that might affect your business plans. For example, if you want to know what type of firm to acquire or merge with, it would make sense to know where these firms are located and how their own business plans may have changed due to industry trends. These trends are disruptive, which leads to opportunity.

These changes are rippling across the industry and creating chaos as one firm sells out to another only to be bought out by a bigger firm. On May 16, 2019, for example, a major New York investment bank made an incredible announcement; they bought a private wealth management firm for $750 million. These buyouts can create many concerned advisors who feel alienated by the new culture, and therein lies a big opportunity. This is an opening, in Japanese called *kyo*, that presents itself if you know how to play the long game and take advantage of others' mistakes.

This major opportunity is created when all these changes, like compensation, compliance, and operations, cascade down on the industry and force the advisor to rethink their whole business model and what firm they want to work with or work for. Thousands of firms are affected by these corporate changes, and that's why I want to introduce you to Brett Flint. He is exactly the type of executive that orchestrates these changes and reads the tea leaves of where the industry is headed.

For reasons of privacy, I have changed the name of the CEO and some of the facts to keep this regional firm anonymous.

When you first meet Brett, you might think he is from the Midwest and that he is ex-military. You would be wrong on both counts. He is from the South and has such focus and discipline that you immediately think "ex-military" or "counterintelligence." He is tall and has a warm, affable smile but a deep and focused look as he engages you in conversation. Brett is a deep thinker that plans for the long term and can articulate that vision very well.

He is now president and CEO of a regional broker-dealer and senior vice president of distribution at a small life insurance company. Brett had extensive prior experience at two other well-known national investment firms that really primed him for this new and exciting opportunity.

IDENTITY CRISIS

When Brett was hired by this broker-dealer in July of 2015, he knew he was with a firm in the middle of an "identity crisis." To management's credit, they knew there were challenges and inconsistencies within their broker-dealer network, and that's why they hired Brett. He had to "define where they were and put a stake in the ground" regarding the advisors they would work with moving forward.

This is a firm that was thirty-plus years old, and I had to help define where we want to be to compete effectively in the marketplace.

When he arrived at the securities firm, they were supporting a mishmash of over 1,100 advisors spread across different industries and different time zones. They were supporting RIAs, OSJs, and insurance distributors along with registered reps themselves. As Brett notes, "we had to evangelize the brand" and really focus on what advisors and what markets they wanted to remain in while deftly pruning the 1,100 down to an eventual cohesive group of about 650 over a three-year time period. His initial audience was predominantly the life and annuity PPGA (Personal Producing General Agency) system. As he finished explaining this to me, the analogy that ran through my head was too good to ignore.

After I graded for and passed my black belt after four years of training in the early 1980s, I was asked by a senior instructor to fill in and teach an adult karate class. I thought, "Piece of cake." As I completed the warm-ups and scanned the class of twenty or so students, it hit me instantly. I had to teach white belts, green belts, and brown belts all at the same time, despite the fact that they had different skill levels and needs. This was going to be more challenging than I thought.

The white belts (beginners) needed the most attention, direction, and feedback, for obvious reasons. Green belts needed similar attention, but more emphasis now on refining technique and the ability to self-correct to some degree. The brown belts, some of whom would be taking the very same black belt exam I had just passed, needed more coaching on power and speed. Moreover, brown belts needed more technical corrections on some key aspects of their favorite kata (forms). With so many moving parts, it was initially overwhelming for me to teach that first class.

The life insurance agents could be viewed as white belts when it comes to the securities industry because they lack the expertise in the areas of stocks, bonds, mutual funds, and real estate investment trusts (REITs). The beginning financial advisor who does not yet do comprehensive planning is like the green belt who needs direction and guidance. The experienced advisor who wants to grow into wealth management and acquisitions is like the brown belt who is training for the black belt exam. Brett needed to integrate all the various skill levels and product lines for both the insurance agents and the advisors.

He knew his mission wouldn't be easy, but one of the main advantages he had was with his bosses. *"We had autonomy but alignment. We had the freedom to execute."* This meant he was free to move about the proverbial financial chessboard as long as the alignment, the goal, was consistent. His first move was to help the securities firm become a pure independent broker-dealer supporting independent advisors. This is the exact trajectory my career path took when I started with a Massachusetts--based insurance company in 1990. That meant the life insurance agents and the PPGA career paths were not so critical to the future of this securities firm.

DE-RISKING

As you can imagine, in the beginning, it was scary and frustrating. The new "technology platform" was more complex and all of the advisors (representatives) had to be informed of the new direction the company was moving in. One crucial decision was who to focus on. After reviewing trends in the marketplace, the life insurance company wanted to focus on wealth advisors and financial planners (the green belts and brown belts) who are by their very nature long-term focused, not the transaction-oriented brokers (the white belts or insurance agents). Once again, another opportunity to improve financial performance.

This was the equivalent of a "buy and hold" strategy versus a "day trading" mentality. The revenue of the firm initially took a big hit; they wanted to preserve the top talent yet be kind and sympathetic to those advisors who would not be with them in the future. He had to be professional and polite. This term was coined internally as "de-risking." In other words, with fewer overall advisors and a more focused approach on planning, management streamlined and "de-risked" the sales force at the same time.

As they continued to prune the ranks of the advisors, allowing for some of them to change course and stay with the life insurance company, a funny thing happened. The profitability climbed tremendously after these changes, and they refined where they wanted to go moving forward. This new strategy opened up new opportunities. Now the focus has shifted to acquisitions (hence the title of this book), which represented an 8–9 percent growth rate that was previously nonexistent. With such a large sales force being pruned, that left opportunities for players to merge with their peers and stay within the current system.

Brett noted, *"There continues to be an express interest in advice-linked Assets Under Management (AUM), and the premium associated with those assets is trading at a high multiple these days, and that is just a function of the supply/demand characteristics in the marketplace."* Brett is referring to the overwhelming imbalance of buyers and sellers. By some estimates, there are forty to fifty buyers for each seller in the marketplace today. Brett added, "It is a bit frothy now. You have RIAs and advisors who are looking to fully or partially monetize their business, and those businesses have been steeply linked to the equity markets, which are at all-time highs, given the ten year bull market we have been in. But not all buyers are experts at this game either."

Because of this success, they have also added a new form of growth that the industry calls "equity participation." This is a new direction for the financial services industry. Bingo, another opportunity. Basically, the life insurance company will loan an RIA money for that firm to go out and do acquisitions. This is what I am personally doing with my own firm, but in my case, on a much smaller scale. I am that brown belt from years ago that became the advanced black belt in this M&A game.

Once the RIA has a loan from this life insurance company, they can go out and buy other firms that fit into the strategic mold that Brett and his team helped create when they went through the de-risking process. This is a smart move, which allows for more explosive growth. Basically, this life insurance company can recruit the exact type of advisor they want, even one with a large client base. Then they help that new advisor with loans so that client (advisor or RIA) goes out to find more firms that fit the strategic mold. Clearly this strategy can lead to exponential growth, and it has already started.

The story gets better, because with all this chaos, even more opportunity is created. Just as the insurance company can grow their own sales force, so will many other broker-dealers and investment firms by following the same strategy. And here is the kicker, all those life insurance agents, advisors, or planners who are not thrilled by this new order are now talking to firms like mine in order to craft a better future or their own exit strategy. The chaos continues to lead to new opportunities, and the cycle will continue as the aging wave of advisors seeks to find the best alternative available.

KEY ACTION STEPS/TAKEAWAYS

1. During times of critical change, autonomy and alignment with top management are critical components of success.

2. Don't assume that the overwhelming imbalance of buyers to sellers (fifty to one) implies no good deals are available or that every buyer is an expert.

3. Check with your RIA or broker-dealer to see if they will loan you money at attractive rates to buy other firms.

CHAPTER 9

MIKE HURST—ONE ADVISOR'S JOURNEY TO RETIREMENT

———

"Those who seek the easy way do not seek the true way."

—DOGEN ZENJI

I want to share a personal story with you about one of my most revealing acquisitions. It is one of my favorite acquisitions because it has a rhythm and a flow that seemed more natural, yet it was not without its tense moments. Mike is in his mid-seventies, tall, broad-shouldered, with gray hair and glasses, and his posture has a slight stoop, leaning forward as if he was going to tell you a closely guarded secret. He is gregarious, humorous, and kind, like a grandfather right out of central casting in Hollywood. His career most certainly did not start out the easy way.

My career started in failure due to a nine-year marriage in my late twenties that was less than ideal. In fact, it was awful. When the divorce was over, it took eighteen months to put my life back together again. I took insurance courses to start off. I had been an insurance adjuster, so I knew some of the ropes. I took a job with a company that allowed me to advance quickly, and I worked hard and then went as far as I could and had to move on.

Mike went through a few organizations and found out the hard way that "not everybody in the financial services world is completely honest." Some places he couldn't get out of fast enough. He found a home with a major New England life insurance company and enjoyed that program. In one training class, they told him, "When you sell someone a mutual fund or an investment product or an annuity, then you're done. You move on to the next prospect."

"I sat there and thought to myself, 'This is not the way it is supposed to be.'" Mike made a mental note: he wanted to be different, better, but it would not be easy.

Early in his career, in the early to mid-1980s, he made up his mind. Mike did what many other successful people do when they are playing the long game, they do things differently. He was going to do what other advisors were not doing.

"I was going to be proactive with my clients. Plain and simple, I would be there for them."

THE COMMISSION ERA

This was the era before advisory fees—or ongoing compensation, as we call it—kicked in. Mike would get a commission if he sold a product, but he couldn't make a change until he got the client's permission, which is still called nondiscretionary authority. In those days, almost all trades were nondiscretionary. More importantly, he wouldn't get paid for making those trades, nor did he want to. He was simply putting the client first as he always did. If he was an actor in an old western movie, he would be one of the guys wearing a white cowboy hat.

One of Mike's favorite expressions that he picked up along the way is: *"Basically, there are two kinds of people: those that do as much as they can, and those that do as little as they can get away with."* He knew that phrase resonated with his clients, and they understood he was always going to be the former, never the latter. Many of his clients had experiences with other agents or planners who never really followed up with their promises. Mike's frustration was that the whole industry operated this way; that is, just tell the clients to stay the course and never make changes to the portfolio.

The industry phrase is known as "set it and forget it," meaning you put the client in a prearranged model and forget about it. Another common phrase to keep the client in the portfolio for the long term was "You have to be in it to win it." That means you have to be fully invested in the market at all times to "win" the game of investing, to make money and grow your portfolio.

Mike continues, "If everybody doesn't do anything, then nobody is wrong for doing nothing." Therefore, in a bear market or a bad market, most advisors don't reallocate their clients' money to protect them, even though the advisors may have told the clients they would take care of them in tough times. "My aspect was 'People are putting money in the market to make money, they need to make money, that is where their retirement is going to come from. They think they're getting help, but they're not.' I was going to be the one that would give them that help."

Mike was very blunt and direct with his clients from the first meeting about the realities of the business and the markets. "One of the smart things I did was to say, 'I make decisions every day, some days I do nothing, other days I make moves. I know before I start that not every move will be right. Nobody makes the right move all the time. There will be times that I am wrong.' I was very up-front with that with all my clients." He tried to clearly set expectations that they should not expect him to be right all the time.

His thesis was that every security can be the best holding in the world, up to a certain date. "If I got to the time when that security was not a good security anymore, for whatever reason, then if that was the time to get out, I did it. Everyone else (advisors) would hang in there and not make changes and still charge a management fee to watch over the portfolio." As he puts it so eloquently, *"I would want to be for my clients what I would want someone to be for me. If I gave someone my money and something went wrong, I would want them to tell me what to do. And if there is an opportunity out there, I would hope the advisor would call me and say, 'Here is something to take advantage of.'"* His only challenge: there was never enough time to do everything he wanted to do for his clients. No matter how efficient he tried to be, it was always a difficult task to stay on top of everything.

Another dirty industry secret was that many agents and advisors would get lazy and make changes just to get paid. One term used was churning, but the term Mike heard was "harvesting." Just to be clear, the old term for harvesting meant the advisor was working his book of business by switching all of his clients from one mutual fund company to another and getting paid for it. Mike knew back then that this was either outrightly illegal or certainly unethical. That was the easy way to make money, not the right way.

The better move, the harder way, would be to exchange from one mutual fund in the same family to another one in the same family with no charge to the client and no additional revenue to the advisor. When his firm brought in an outside speaker about a new product, Mike was always the guy sitting in the front row trying to absorb it all and learn about a new annuity product or life insurance twist. "I was obsessive about learning everything and taking care of my clients."

As his career progressed, he would read the *Wall Street Journal* daily, keep up with TV news, and attend meetings and conferences. Always absorbing, always learning. He particularly liked the American Funds conferences. "I never missed one of those conferences." Mike was always trying to connect the dots and learn how one thing affected another. In the early 1990s, he switched to another firm, a broker-dealer, to move away from the life insurance industry. He did not like what the general agent was doing with agents' money and did not have a lot of faith in how he managed the local agency. He asked around about other firms and found out about a firm near the Boston area.

Mike literally hopped in his car and drove two hours east to the company's headquarters unannounced, and they were so surprised and caught off guard that they stuck him in with other prearranged recruits that day and he tagged along for the presentations. He got a better payout and met some nice people. He liked their philosophy about how they did business and especially enjoyed his contacts with the compliance department.

As Mike proudly states, "I was always doing what compliance personnel wanted you to do for the most part, but never demanded that you do." The advisory business was just starting to take off in the early to mid-nineties. Mike was doing all the work that a fee-based advisor would eventually do without any compensation at the time. This emphasis on research, detailed work, and thorough analysis was exhausting at times, and he felt that "I cannot do my job right if I don't do the research. I put strong limitations on how fast I could grow my client base." Mike did acknowledge the other side to that coin: all the time put into research could have been put into finding new clients. The same enemy was still lurking in the shadows: time.

FEE-BASED REVOLUTION

When the advisory revolution started off, the minimum account sizes were at least $25,000. So an advisor that had client accounts under $25,000 had to keep doing things the old way: more time-consuming and less efficient. The new accounts, called "advisory accounts" allowed the advisor to make moves without calling the client (discretionary authority) and without charging commissions (hence the term "fee-based"). The advisor received compensation quarterly based on the size of the account. As the accounts grew in size, so did the revenue. This was the true way, the best way, to manage money.

As the fee-based revolution continued, especially after markets like the 2000–2003 tech wreck, it became obvious that clients could be better off paying an annual management fee to their advisor. If the advisor had the integrity of people like Mike, then allowing the advisor to make changes "on the fly" and without client permission each time gave the advisor timelier flexibility to adapt to changing market conditions. Voilà! Now the client and the advisor are on the same side of the table, because each time an advisor trades, they are not generating a commission, they are simply trying to rebalance the client's account(s) to meet their short- and long-term objectives. He then transitioned his book of business to a fee-based environment, one client at a time, as he conducted his meetings in 2002 and after. Most clients did transfer to the new account type, but some still held on to the old way. I personally did this with my entire client base in almost the exact same time frame.

During the 2008–2009 financial crisis, Mike had even more clients to take care of. To put it into perspective, 2000–2003 was a three-year bear market, down double digits three years in a row. That time period was the worst stock market period since the Great Depression, but "2008 was worse than that. And it happened in a shorter time frame." Once again, the mantra of buy and hold was not the right recommendation (according to Mike) and we were "days away from an entire worldwide financial collapse" and telling clients to "just hold on" was "probably not a good idea." Once again, he got even more referrals, and he finally had enough time to just focus on his current clients. He was spending even less time taking on new clients and put another limitation on the size of his business. "The clients were pleased—I was happy with that. Taking responsibility is something you pay the price for, because you are not always right and you cannot avoid making a wrong decision." But he was starting to win the war of attrition with his nemesis, time.

SUCCESSION-PLANNING JOURNEY

In 2011, Mike was somewhat blindsided when a client, a top executive at a major aerospace company, asked him if he had a succession plan. "I was never thinking about retirement, just focusing on what I wanted to do and the way I wanted to do it. And this planted a seed in my mind that kept coming up. And as I stopped to think about it, the realization hit me that I can't do this forever." Mike thinks the client was thinking more about Mike's welfare and personal retirement rather than injecting any concern about Mike's ability to continue to be a competent planner. That shows you how much his clients cared for him.

Mike was still battling his old enemy, time; he had kids finishing college and many other things up in the air. But that same client explained to Mike that Mike's revenue was ongoing and recurring, and there should be value in that. That thought stuck in Mike's brain. It was a slow process that dawned on him over time.

At one of his next annual conferences, he attended a talk by FP Transitions. Now he started to look at a whole new world of succession planning, and why not start with his current firm? Two years later, around the spring of 2013, he started to look more seriously into the succession-planning process. "Some days I think I can do this forever, but there are some days I can't get out fast enough because of the stress." I have personally witnessed this statement from many dozens of advisors over the years. Ron Carson calls this cohort "rich and tired."

When an advisor first makes a decision about retiring or creating a succession plan, he or she has a lot of different options.

Many thoughts run through your head at the same time: Do I pick a firm already within my broker-dealer? Do I pick a firm that is local, regardless of the back-office affiliation? One of the most important decisions is the philosophy of the other firm, the culture, and the owner. Do those characteristics match up, or mesh, with your current thinking? And sometimes, as in Mike's case, he got a call from a firm that was looking to acquire his firm and become his succession plan. That firm, though, was out of state and not in his same broker-dealer.

He thought the out-of-state firm might not work because of the distance, but this important call started him on his journey. Just maybe he was finally gaining on his archenemy: time. As luck would have it, he kept talking to his contacts at his home office, also in Massachusetts, when one day the person on the other end of the phone said, "I want to buy your practice—will you sell it to me?"

"This was easy, all I have to do is wait for an offer, and then I'll be done," thought Mike. It looked very easy, but looks can be deceiving.

Mike followed up later that year, around 2012, to the same individual at the home office. That individual told Mike bad news: the parent company had been sold, and he was being offered a job with the new company at the same headquarters, leaving Mike in a pickle. After hearing about this new opportunity, Mike did what he always did: he put his friend first when he said, "If it were me, I'd take that job." Mike was telling his first and best potential buyer to take the salary offer and not buy Mike's business. Once again, the true way, the honest way, was not the easy way.

When that door closed, another one opened up, this time even better. Another financial representative at the same firm, but closer geographically to his office, reached out with what seemed a realistic plan. The advisor put a whole new office space together within weeks and asked Mike to come in and bring his files. Mike thought that was a red flag, since there was no written agreement and not even a hint of a draft at this point. Moreover, the advisor wanted to have some meetings with Mike and Mike's clients in the new offices. Red flag number two.

Mike kept thinking, "We don't have an agreement, and the clients would get confused. I was naive," Mike added. He waited for months for a draft, some type of agreement, and it never happened. While Mike was waiting for a reply from the advisor, he went to FP Transitions and paid for a valuation report to put on the advisor's desk. Mike was patiently waiting for the reply. He thought for sure this not-so-subtle gesture would finally start a real conversation about price, terms, and value. And then a flashback from Mike's own family came soaring through his frontal lobe.

Mike recalled a story from one of his favorite cousins, Jim, who was well past retirement age and in a similar business when that cousin decided to put a plan together to sell his business. Jim thought he'd found a good candidate, agreed to let the candidate interview him, and provided confidential information that was intended to be used as part of a valuation proposal. Jim was also naive and trusted this individual before any documents were signed.

The next thing Jim knows, this person starts soliciting Jim's clients: he knew the prices and the client profiles, and "he was cherry-picking everything in sight." Mike continued his story with me and said, "It occurred to me, 'This is probably going to happen to me if I stay with this guy and follow his lead.'" Two times this thing hasn't worked, two red flags, and Mike knew he had to leave. Mike wasn't waiting around for a third strike. He received one more email from this phony buyer trying to set up another meeting. Mike replied, "That won't be necessary." He sifted through more calls and leads, even remembering that he and I had spoken, with a brief office visit, almost two years prior to this moment. But the out-of-state location still scared him.

IRS FORM 8594

Mike went back to the drawing board and started working with other contacts and other candidates. Among some of his lessons here? One buyer couldn't come up with the financing, and another buyer tried to play games with the capital gains assumption on the final offer. That buyer essentially said, "You fill in whatever numbers you want on IRS form 8594. I'll do what my accountant tells me." Was this buyer delusional or some distant cousin of Al Capone? Mike knew that "the IRS doesn't work this way. They're looking at both sides of that coin to make sure everyone is on the same wavelength."

In other words, the buyer and seller can't put in different numbers for capital gains on the same transaction. The numbers have to match. Finally, he went to FP Transitions and let them market it for him. He had lots of productive conversations and sifted and sorted through all the discussions. "It was of primary importance that the clients be well taken care of." As he continued to meet different buyers, he thought he met the final buyer near Boston, Massachusetts, and was ready to go ahead until he got one more call. That call was from me. That changed everything.

Mike made one more visit with me, and after I ranted and raved about how good my firm was, he gave in and told the other guy in eastern Massachusetts that he found a buyer in Connecticut. That buyer was me. We laugh about it now. The advice he was given from FP Transitions was to look at two angles: "Which advisor is best for the clients? Which advisor is best for you?" Then Mike had his answer: he went with the advisor that was best for the clients and best for him. I was proud that my team made such a positive impression on him during his second and third visits. When the sale was complete, I said, "You're going to love it. You will love this process."

Mike was a bit nervous because he wanted the transition to work for both of us. "I will do everything I can to make it work." Would the clients accept the new owner? It turns out they did. These clients were his friends, and they were happy Mike was retiring. They were happy for *him*. That was a new feeling for Mike. And the distance was never an issue in the end, because his clients were saying, "We trust you, Mike. If you trust this firm in Connecticut, then we rely on your good judgment." Together with my team, we scheduled over thirty-five meetings with Mike, me, and/or one of my associates at every single meeting. This was the honest way, the best way, to have both buyer and seller present at client meetings.

Mike was never known as a guy that shows lots of emotion. He was not a touchy-feely type of guy. But something was different now. He was hugging his clients during this transition. "I never hugged anybody. I was never a hugger." It was such a great ambience, it seemed natural for everyone to start hugging. Since it was a bull market, I could not describe them as "bear hugs."

A few weeks after the transition was complete, he was in church one day and saw the minister approach him. He knew the minister well because Mike was a founding member of the church bereavement committee. As the minister approached with a smile, he asked Mike how he was doing. Mike replied with a big smile, "Ebullient." Mike continued, "I have so much more time to do the things I want to do, and my clients are in great hands." He even started writing his own book.

Mike had finally defeated his mortal enemy, time. He had enough time now and for the rest of his life.

There is a certain karma in this that seems well deserved. The true way, the honest way, was the best way.

KEY ACTION STEPS/TAKEAWAYS

1. Seeking the easy way out, in all things, does not build long-term sustainability.

2. Set realistic expectations with your clients. Someday when you sell your firm, the new owner can piggyback on that solid foundation.

3. Script your retirement years before you retire. Work on a theme of the major goals you want to achieve or the hobbies and activities you want to spend your free time on.

CHAPTER 10

STEVE—ARCHETYPE OF A DIFFICULT ACQUISITION

"There is no error greater than hatred. And nothing mightier than patience. So I strive in every way to learn patience."

—BUDDHA

Do you have patience in your life? Do you have patience in your business?

In a book about business acquisitions, you might not expect to find a whole chapter devoted to a challenging acquisition. Yet many of us, including myself, would acknowledge there are plenty of minefields in the M&A space. Moreover, learning from failure is a very sensible approach: why not learn from other's mistakes when it costs you nothing? Therefore, I wanted to draw your attention to a classic type of failed acquisition that is more common than you think. This same scenario happened to me personally as well as friends of mine across the country whom I've met through various coaching programs. You might want to call it the "blinders on" mentality, but I prefer to call it "the paucity of patience" scenario.

When one first starts to look at buying a company (and even if you are selling), we tends to get so motivated, excited, optimistic, and impatient that one overlooks the warning signs, red flags, and flashing blue lights. I can think of at least two reasons why I made this very mistake, and I will share a story of an advisor scenario that will help make this clear.

Steve (not his real name) is one of my business coaches that has helped me immensely over the years, and he was relating a story from two years ago about a very contentious acquisition he was attempting to salvage. Steve has coached advisors for nearly as long as I have been in the business, over thirty years. We both agreed on two key issues right off the bat.

First and foremost, the vast majority of the advisors I have met or spoken to are positive, upbeat, optimistic people. Therefore, we generally don't interpret early warning signs as dangers; we look at them as obstacles to overcome. After all, that's how many of us became successful: we overcame the odds, bucked the trends, and fought through adversity. Yet the one factor that new buyers and sellers lack is *patience*. When I was working on my first few acquisitions, my due diligence period would last a few days (instead of weeks or months now), and I was ready to write a check and move forward way too soon. Now my team and I have a process that is repeatable, flexible, and sustainable.

Second, as Steve eloquently puts it, "You should not be out there in the M&A world looking for lost puppies to save. You can be kind and caring as an advisor, but don't go chasing lost puppies. Especially lost puppies that don't want to change and adapt to the future." In other words, many advisors are kind to a fault. They want to please people, just the way they have been pleasing their clients for their entire career. I also made this mistake many years ago on one of my earlier acquisitions. Steve has this gem of a quote. "The best deals you make are the (bad) ones you never do." In other words, avoiding the mistakes, the bad deals, can be much more profitable than landing a good deal.

In this particular transaction, Steve did not introduce the buyer to the seller; he merely tried to lend assistance as this situation spun out of control. I will summarize the key aspects of this failed acquisition and if you get nothing else from this book except the ideas of patience and perseverance,

I will consider the book a success. One very successful player in this business who wished to remain anonymous gave me a great quote. "Anyone who has a strong personality wants to have success, not succession."

Steve told me that he knew in the first twenty minutes of discussion with the buyer that this would not be easy. Here are some of the important facts:

1. The buyer and seller were located within sixty miles of each other but had never met before this deal. They were both located in well-known Midwestern cities.

2. The buyer and seller worked in different communities, and despite both being from the Midwest, the cultures were as different as Hollywood and Skid Row. While Hollywood and Skid Row are separated by less than ten miles in downtown Los Angeles, their cultures are at opposite ends of the spectrum.

3. The buyer owned an advisory firm with roughly $100 million of fee-based AUM and was a top producer at his broker-dealer.

4. The seller owned a commission-oriented business that generated about $600,000 of GDC (revenue) each year, and it ebbed and flowed over the past few years. Most of

the book was A shares and commission-oriented variable annuities which added up to about $70 million in assets. The seller was also at the same broker-dealer.

5. The buyer was innovative and entrepreneurial while the seller was bored and disengaged.

Now I admit this is an extreme example, but it is based on a real-life scenario, and this same dynamic, with minor variations, plays itself out year after year across the country in the M&A business. Steve continued explaining to me, "I knew from the moment I talked to the buyer that there was a disconnect in this process." First, you have to be cognizant of the different business models, fees versus commission. Second, don't be fooled by a firm that is physically located near you. That can be an advantage, but don't anchor on it. Third, the personalities were markedly different. The acquirer, a fee-oriented advisor, was successful, relaxed, and easygoing, and he and his team had a great service model. They really spoiled their clients with white-glove service. The seller had few friends or acquaintances in the business, even after a thirty-year career.

Clearly, the seller and his firm were not cut from the same cloth. The buyer's clients were used to a white-collar, fiduciary-based advisory world. The seller's clients were in a different business model: no discretionary trading, little advisory business, no financial planning or retirement analysis. Basically, this practice was on autopilot, but the fuel tank gauge was hovering just above the *E* (for empty) on the dashboard. This firm had one administrative assistant who was part-time and not heavily involved. Clients had no unique client experience, no formal annual review process, and client appreciation events were as rare as a Chicago Cubs World Series victory. In short, the service model was like an automated car wash without the water.

So what was the driver, or enticement, for the buyer? Well, as it happens, both firms were in the same broker-dealer. In other words, they had a common connection with the same community of advisors. They shared the same home office and the same custodian. This too is not an uncommon connection, but whether you are part of a large RIA network or a similar community of fee-only planners, don't just anchor on that commonality and forget all the other moving parts. Having a common connection alone is not enough to justify a merger or acquisition.

As Steve says, "There was a lot of misalignment from day one. Different people from different communities with different personalities." How would the seller ever get behind and sell the concept of this buyer and his white-glove service? And if the seller was disengaged to start with, what would motivate him to endorse a new business model that was superior to his and potentially embarrassing to his staff? The seller was an old dinosaur who didn't want to change and had no patience with adapting to the new world order.

Now imagine how difficult it is for a seller who doesn't believe in a value-added model with high-service, high-touch client experience to convey that story to his clients. A famous quote (some attribute this to Confucius) reads, *"One who chases after two hares won't catch even one."* Another variation reads, "A man who chases two rabbits catches neither." Either way, you get the point: trying to go after two different business models by chasing a seller who has a different mind-set than yours will only end in frustration. The seller won't have the patience to listen to and adapt a new business model. The buyer thinks that it will be easy to convert the clients once the seller is retired and out of the business. That's why you need patience, especially early on, to evaluate all aspects of the potential deal before jumping in.

But things got worse. The seller, who had a blue-collar client base with no service model, thought that the buyer was wasting his time and spending way too much time and money on the white-glove service model. In fact, the seller thought of his own firm as a cash cow and had no intention of reinvesting money and taking care of clients at a high level. The buyer talked himself into buying this practice, which was more of a "warm prospect list" than an actual investment firm. The deal structure was simple: a 40 percent cash down payment and the remaining amount, the other 60 percent, was on a note payable over five years. In addition, the buyer thought that getting a small discount would make the deal work. So instead of paying 1.5 times the trailing twelve months revenue, the buyer thought that getting it for 1.2 times trailing twelve months was a steal. It was not.

During the actual transition, the seller was so uninvested in the new environment that the administrative assistant from the seller was doing all the communication with the buyer and the majority of communication with the seller's clients. This is not the way a deal should work out. The assistant was pushing the seller (her boss) to agree to let her set the meetings, review the talking points, and push the process forward. Also, don't forget that the assistant to the seller was very conflicted, because if she was working with the buyer to set meetings, that very act often conflicted with the seller's way of doing business. The most damaging statistic of all was the transition speed of the top fifty clients: as of five months into the acquisition, only twenty of the top fifty clients had been met in person. If the buyer had thought through, with patience, all the red flags and inconsistencies, this disaster could have been avoided.

In case you thought things couldn't unravel anymore, I saved the best for last. During the transition process, the seller actually suggested to some of his clients that the management fee charged by the buyer was too high! You read that right. The seller was sabotaging the whole deal, and the financial penalty for doing so was not a deterrent. The purchase and sale agreement did have some clauses, or clawbacks, that involved a loss of money to the buyer if a certain percentage of clients did not remain with the buyer. However, if those clauses "don't have enough teeth," as Steve says, then you automatically set yourself up for potential disaster. Because that's when the lawyers get involved.

So it is crucial to take your time, evaluate all the aspects of a deal with a checklist, get input from those you trust, and don't be afraid to walk away.

In short, we can borrow a great phrase from Warren Buffet. "The stock market is a device for transferring money from the impatient to the patient."

Just make sure you are the one being patient.

KEY ACTION STEPS/TAKEAWAYS:

1. Failed acquisitions can often be spotted in advance if there is a cultural misfit. "Culture eats strategy for lunch," as Ron Carson says.

2. Forget trying to save "lost puppies." Your job is not to rescue, resuscitate, or revive a potential acquisition target.

3. "The best deals you make are the (bad) ones you never do."

PART 5

FINALIZING
THE DEAL

CHAPTER 11

POST SIGNING—THE ART OF INTEGRATION

———

"When it is obvious that the goals cannot be reached, don't adjust the goals, adjust the action steps."

—CONFUCIUS

A well written book on the M&A business wouldn't be complete without at least one chapter that focuses on not just the goal of an acquisition but some of the common obstacles and adjustments that must be made to make the acquisition a reality. To make it a successful reality. Often-times, top management may set some aggressive acquisition goals that are not realistic, at least for the rank and file, yet the feedback loop never quite makes its way back to the

C-suite. This is a mistake. Sometimes the action steps need to be adjusted.

One key corporate function that has eyes and ears across the entire spectrum of acquisitions is HR or human resources. For those of you that may not have worked in this area, HR has many touch points throughout most larger organizations. For example, the HR team needs to know early on what staffing levels would be required for a new acquisition. What skill set is necessary to integrate this new business? Are there labor laws that need to be addressed or double-checked? Are there contracts to be negotiated up front? Who in legal or accounting will be spearheading the due diligence process? What about the needs of the IT or CIO functional areas that are affected by this new potential acquisition? The list goes on and on. That's why I wanted to introduce you to Dan, who knows these waters like a seasoned guide.

For reasons of confidentiality, I have changed his name and a few minor details, but all the facts and the story line are taken directly from the interview.

Dan is a veteran human resources executive with over twenty-five years of HR experience in consulting, financial services, academia, supply chain management, health care, and technology. The focus of this chapter is his experience in the supply chain management role, although his wisdom is from all his prior functional assignments. Dan excelled at this role for over five years while working for the CEO, founder, and owner of this privately held firm. He worked on over a dozen acquisitions during his tenure.

GAZELLE

I will give the supply chain company a fictitious name for ease of discussion: Gazelle (not the internet company). Gazelle had a very aggressive strategy that was focused on growth, primarily through acquisitions. Gazelle wanted to literally jump over all the competition and gobble up the marketplace and gain market share. Just as in real life, while a gazelle can run at speeds up to 60 mph, they still have natural predators.

Instead of lions, leopards, and cheetahs, Gazelle has competitors with names like Amazon, SuperValu, and Kroger.

The industry that Gazelle competes in is made up of hundreds of mom-and-pop companies, supply chain companies, and large retail chains. The industry is not known for high operating margins: 1–2 percent is a typical number and 3–4 percent would be considered a very good year. As such, high volume of sales and a very efficient operation is essential to its success. Thus, the intuitive goal of continually seeking out acquisitions makes sense.

Gazelle specialized in supply chain efficiency and movement of products. For example, their warehouse operations were among the most efficient in the industry. If a potential deal involved a package of supply chain operations and a retail component, the short-term plan was to sell the retail operation but maintain the contracts with the manufacturers, because that is where the cash flow existed. The contracts were the pot of gold: they were long term and cash-flow positive. Moreover, Gazelle wanted to maintain a relationship with the eventual buyer of the retail business. Gazelle's management approached the industry with a swagger like "We're bigger, we're better, we're smarter, and we can take what you already have and make it better." The question was, Better for who?

Dan and his team normally got involved after the LOI (letter of intent) was signed. The first key step is to form the integration team, because they conduct further due diligence along with planning, execution, and valuation work that helps refine the process. This is where action steps would need to be adjusted in order to make the goal a reality. Top management wanted the team to "make this work on a certain timeline." Sometimes the deadline was very tight. Dan's team was like a standby medevac team on red alert, defibrillators in hand, ready to go on a moment's notice. Half of the time, the deal was already signed when they got the call, but the other half they would get the chance to assess how Gazelle would integrate culture on the supply chain side. His team's focus was normally on culture and integration.

Again, this is exactly where the action steps would be modified. For example, if Dan's team felt a need for town hall meetings with the new employees in order to communicate corporate philosophy, this action step would be added in the beginning. He explained to me, "We learned that having these early and often helped the process go smoother rather than waiting until the end of the process." There was continuous and ongoing communication along with a detectivelike focus on the day-to-day operations.

There were many moving parts, and like a conveyor belt, day-to-day operations were not halted while the new systems were being assessed. One classic example was software: Gazelle had to determine very quickly if this newly acquired software was better than their current corporate software, or if not, whether it could be merged into an existing program. The rank-and-file staffing usually remained steady, whereas the G&A (general and administrative) functions were often duplicated and thus candidates for elimination. Once again, the speed of this conveyor belt was so fast after a deal closed, there was a real need for a steady flow of meetings to bring the teams together. Long-term employees from the acquired company felt their world was turned upside down. Adjusting the action steps would allow them time to acclimatize to the new environment.

The goal was to save money by eliminating redundant positions and overlapping departments. Regardless of how many acquisitions you complete, you still have to make each one profitable enough to justify the time, effort, and resources allocated to that deal. Gazelle created financial models before the deal was signed in order to track the progress toward the goal. The sooner Gazelle could realize the synergies, the more profitable the deal would become. When Dan explained their process to me, it reminded me of an online ad I saw recently. A company will collect your favorite old T-shirts, cut them up, and stitch them back as one big quilt. It is popular for college-bound students to roll all their memories into one usable quilt. The end result is impressive, but the process is not so elegant.

Many of the G&A functions that Gazelle acquired (finance, accounting, IT) were almost eliminated or cut entirely and absorbed by corporate functions right away. Again, if the deal was moving too fast because the goal was aggressive, Gazelle had to make adjustments along the way. They might hold on to an accounting department a bit longer until all the loose ends are tied up and the books reconcile properly. In addition, if a newly acquired warehouse had some great inventory software that Gazelle had not known about, they would allow that inventory control system to run parallel with their own until they could decide which program was superior and worth keeping.

CULTURAL CLASHES

Cultural clashes happened despite all the town hall meetings and employee educational sessions. The biggest clash was over the length of the work day. Gazelle imposed their corporate work ethic and culture on these newly acquired firms. According to Dan, the mantra was "'We're going to do whatever it takes to meet our customers' needs and demands.' That usually meant management may have worked eight hours per day before the deal, but people would find their workweeks increasing in hours worked. That is our style."

Gazelle wanted to be the biggest, and the way to meet that goal is to own all the contracts (cash flow) by snapping up all the competitors. This is the corporate equivalent of Sherman's "scorched earth" policy through Georgia in the fall of 1864. You win the battle, but what is the ultimate price you pay to squeeze all the juice out of the lemon?

At times, it seemed as if management did not care too much about the culture of the firm they were acquiring. Perhaps the brand or reputation of some of the deals were important, but it was important to Gazelle that corporate was quick to "rebrand our name on everything" after the deal was complete unless they were going to continue to operate by the prior company's name for customer continuity. The thinking was that "people will have to come around to our way of doing business." But if the goal was to grow through acquisitions and integrate these new employees properly, then surely culture would play a role in the overall well-being of the combined companies.

There was one exception when it came to adjusting the action steps in an acquisition: when the business they were acquiring was a slightly different business than the supply chain business. They bought a technology business and made an effort to maintain the existing culture. It seemed successful, but there was still turnover. The industry itself had high turnover anyway, so management felt it didn't matter if there was some collateral turnover as part of every deal. Employees did not like the new work schedules and changes in policies. One big drawback, employees felt they were working harder with similar pay. That's just the way it was in this high-volume, low-margin business.

The desire to have a smooth, successful cultural transition and integration didn't matter as much as "getting the deal done." Dan's team at Gazelle did make some improvements though. They got better at completing the transition with the newly acquired company in a hundred days or less, mainly through employee meetings or streamlining existing procedures. Many of these transactions or acquisitions were fairly large in size. Dan did some side math while we were on the phone interview and estimated the deals were between 5 percent and 10 percent of the total revenue of the entire company.

Were there key indicators to know it was successful? Did it work? Sales was the key metric.

POST-CLOSING SALES WAS THE KEY METRIC

Sales was always the most important metric. If sales did not decrease in the first hundred days after an acquisition, that was a good metric. They would talk to every single customer of the newly acquired firm to ensure the sales were maintained. In most cases, they could generate new business along the way. This was a vital action step toward the main goal of preserving revenue. Unlike other steps that might have been rushed, this one was the glue that held everything together. Talking to every single customer and getting their concerns, their feedback, and their perspective was of utmost importance.

There was a big advantage in partnering for volume discounts through the manufacturers, having inventory available for customers, and diversifying the overall product lines. They also added the new employees on the HR and payroll system. That would also include a performance management system. From a labor standpoint, they would review any labor union and contract issues. Management tried hard not to acquire firms that had a large labor union presence. But they would meet with all the labor representatives and employees about the benefits, the performance management program, and any other incentives that they would offer. These road shows would cover the new benefit and retirement programs, which often were much better than the other firm had in place.

Once a firm was bought and was absorbed into overall operations, no one looked back at how the deals looked six or twelve months later. Those companies need to be integrated quickly, meet the financial models, and become part of the vast network of operations in order to succeed. Many acquired operations learned from the parent company in a positive way. Other deals would struggle with change management, cultural differences, or senior leadership that would need to evolve or eventually transition out.

Gazelle was growing so fast and adding so many companies, it seemed as if they didn't care or it didn't matter if an acquired company didn't mesh right away with Gazelle corporate culture. The few deals that did not work out were deals in which the owner did not want to sell or the closely held family business did not want to change their approach. Another deal was nixed because of a price differential of almost $50 million, and that could not be resolved.

Another selling point was the technology that was used in the new facilities. It was too expensive to integrate an older facility with new robotic technology, so firms they bought had to keep using the old technology. In some cases, it was cheaper to build a new facility from the ground up. There was no retrofitting of these older facilities.

They did look at all existing facilities to see if they were close enough to the newly acquired facility, and in a few cases, they could piggyback on that geographical advantage. Some robotic technology was leveraged to be sold to other industries, and that was just in the beginning stages when one of their executives left.

SENIOR MANAGEMENT TURNOVER

Looking back, there has been a lot of turnover at the senior levels of Gazelle over the past few years. The firm has gone through two to three CEOs and many executive vice presidents have resigned or left the firm. They had a family-oriented approach to corporate culture, but that often clashed with the hours or demands of the job. Engagement surveys and culture surveys were always below industry average and getting worse over time.

They were the largest employer in a small town, so there was not much choice of competing jobs; they paid a decent wage and people went to work, did their job, and went home without hanging around. Recruitment of talent to the corporate location was a challenge, and line staff in various locations had high turnover (part of the business). Outside the deal, team, and senior leaders, there didn't seem to be an overriding theme to the acquisitions. No emotion, no slogan, just matter-of-factness. The approach was "This is a target we want to acquire and here are the reasons why. This is what we hope to get out of it, so go, team, go and make it happen." There was no overriding philosophy except "Guys, you have been really successful to date, and we feel we can partner with you and grow both of our businesses." They could have taken their time and added more steps to the process, but that would slow things down.

If you worked in operations or most corporate functions, you were not that impacted by the frenetic pace of acquisitions. But if you were at any senior or executive level for operations or manufacturing or integration teams, you basically had two full-time jobs—your normal day job and your job during the hectic pace of acquisitions. However, while many lives were not impacted during this growth process, "the overall culture and engagement at the senior level was low because it was such a grind of a job."

The philosophy was "I am buying your business so I can get to your customers." Those companies had customers who were locked in contractually through wholesale agreements. The delivery terms and tight schedules to meet were costing more money, customer satisfaction was low, and employees knew about these challenges, so many times, being acquired was a good deal for those customers and employees who needed economies of scale.

Contracts were three to five years in length. They often got to build and manage new relationships that they never would have gotten if they did not buy that firm. Management was successful in growing sales, but revenues were down in part because many of these acquisitions were expensive in terms of land and property that had to be maintained. For example, you still have to maintain insurance on the building, keep the heat on (the Midwest can get very cold in the winter), and of course pay taxes on these structures. "When you don't have people in those buildings yet you are still paying for them— our sales were up, revenues down, and operating margins were hurt by these extra costs." Operating margins are very low in this business, maybe 1–2 percent. "There's not a lot of meat on the bone in this business," and the sunk cost of buildings and land were a significant drag on the bottom line.

Best practices in the M&A world involve conducting a cultural assessment of the organization. Understanding the company's mission, values, and treatment of the workforce are difficult to assess in due diligence. However, it is possible for companies to assess each individual met during the various meetings, the timeliness of response to data requests, and various employees involved in those meetings. That needs to be considered to evaluate gaps with the acquiring company. Once the deal is done and made public—the culture assessment, engagement meetings, and focus groups are essential to monitor the assimilation of employees.

Had these best practices been added, two things for sure would have occurred: One, the process would have taken longer on each deal. Two, and more important, job satisfaction and employee morale would have been much higher. Employee retention would have been much better.

Sometimes you have to slow down to speed up. You don't always have to be the Gazelle. Adjusting the action steps may be painful, but it just might provide a smoother flight and a smoother landing toward your goal.

KEY ACTION STEPS/TAKEAWAYS:

1. HR is a key component, in terms of a culture fit, in many well-run acquisition strategies.

2. Handwrite in advance the pros and cons of any acquisition before the deal is signed. Then check it again throughout the onboarding of the new clients or customers.

3. Do not underestimate the importance of culture when you acquire a company, including aligned management values, first-year expectations, talent assessment, communication, and transparency with the management and employees of the acquired firm.

PART 6

RIA/SERIAL ACQUIRER

CHAPTER 12

RON CARSON—THE FARMER/FINANCIER

———

"One generation plants the tree, and another gets the shade."

—CHINESE PROVERB

I am going to wager that you never thought you would be reading about a farmer in a book on financial services acquisitions. Ron, though, is not your average farmer. Not by a long shot.

First of all, he has an amazing memory; he can recall details about people he met over a decade ago with very little effort. In fact, he told me he never had to work at recalling these details, he acknowledges he was simply born this way and grateful for it. As a matter of fact, right before my telephone interview, he had been at lunch with a couple he met over twelve years ago, and he remembered both their children's and pets' names. The couple was understandably astonished. Moreover, he remembered recently that I was from Boston and into martial arts, although I had not seen him for quite some time, several years in fact.

The other amazing fact is that Ron was trained as an auctioneer in high school. Ron attended a six-week auction school in Kansas City, Missouri, during one of his summer breaks in high school. Ron and his dad had a part-time business that sold consignment items through auctioning. He and his classmates would often walk downtown and practice "crying the auction," which is also known as "bid calling" or "the cattle rattle." Hearing a live auction is an amazing experience if you ever get the chance. Just count your money before you begin bidding!

Ron has the largest farm in Burt County, Nebraska, which is approximately one hour north of Omaha, Nebraska. The county was formed in 1854 and named after Francis Burt, the first governor of the Nebraska Territory. Ron has set some amazing lifetime goals, such as bringing food and water to as many people in third-world countries as possible. He wants to live a utilitarian life. "I want to do the most amount of good for the largest amount of people."

You need to know one more crucial fact about Ron. His namesake firm, Carson Wealth, currently manages more than $10 billion in AUM. As I said above, Ron is not your average farmer.

Because of the farming crisis in the early 1980s, Ron's parents went bankrupt when the FDIC took over the local banks. Ron adapted by changing careers into financial services. He morphed from farmer to financier. That career change was the genesis of Ron's entire wealth management journey, and I suspect those hardships are part of why he gives so much back to the community and to charity.

Ron Carson is a household name in our business, and I was fortunate to meet him in the late 1990s when I joined his coaching program to hone my craft and stay current with industry trends. He is a *New York Times* best-selling author and has published several books about building scalable businesses, most recently *The Sustainable Edge* (2016). Carson Coaching has grown to become one of the leading advisor coaching programs in the country, counting well over twenty thousand advisors and alumni in his program.

I have been in his coaching program for over a decade, and I can't emphasize enough how his teachings and his methodologies have helped me grow my firm and advance my career. In addition, my direct contact at his firm is through my coach

Greg Opitz. Greg has been, and continues to be, an invaluable resource, giving insights into the trends, strategies, and inner workings of the wealth management industry. Carson Group is like a government think tank with metaphorical test tubes and white lab coats, constantly creating or refining the next wave of ideas for the financial services and wealth management industry.

Ron is also a major player in the M&A business, and that is exactly why I wanted to share his thoughts, input, and wisdom with you. His expertise in the M&A world, and the growth of Carson Wealth through acquisitions in particular, was a compelling story I couldn't pass up. After all, you don't grow to $10 billion in assets by just growing soybeans, corn, and beef.

Ron said, "What's important to me is not being the biggest, but it's owning our MTP—massive transformative purpose. We at Carson Group want to be the most trusted for financial advice. If we can own or co-own that space, I will view this endeavor as successful." Ron's definition of MTP is to make huge, radical changes that would transform your business and generate ten times growth. For example, could your own firm of three years ago compete with your firm today? If you answer yes, you really need to consider what action steps would be needed to become massively transformative.

I thought it best to directly share with you below part of the interview.

Q: What is a decision you would go back and change if you could?

A: There are two changes I would have made.

First, I would have surrounded myself with really good people much earlier on in my career. I used to think I had to be the library and know it all. Now I realize I am far better being a librarian. That makes the most sense.

Second, my first M&A deal I ever did was a mistake. I didn't know what I was doing. I underestimated how critical culture is. It was somebody I didn't know that well, and they were a cultural misfit, and it created a lot of friction within my organization. We spend an enormous amount of time now getting the culture right, and we've walked away from numerous deals because there was not cultural alignment. Culture eats strategy for lunch. The best strategies in the world will never be executed if you don't have a good positive, supportive culture.

Q: What has been the biggest surprise in your career?

A: [*nine-second pause*] I never really thought I would have this level of financial success, even to this day. It shocks me that I am where I am at financially. The other big surprise is how hard it is to pull all the pieces together and do it in a really seamless way. The amount of money, time, and talent it has taken to build our ecosystem has shocked me as well. And I don't mean I was off by a factor of two. I mean it was ten times more than what we thought.

Q: What is a failure you are grateful for because you learned from it?

A: Too many to count. But I want to group this one under the Carson family. I am grateful that my parents went broke in 1982. I thought I was going to be a farmer for life before that happened. My sister is a farmer. My parents were farmers. Because of the hardship of my parents going broke, it forced me to take another career path into financial services. The success in financial services allowed me to accumulate money to buy farmland, and this was all the result of a failure that became a blessing.

Q: If you could summarize your career in a word or a phrase, what would it be?

A: A word would be "relentless." A phrase would be "You haven't failed until you quit trying."

Q: What do you see happening in the M&A world right now?

A: It looks frothy right now, but that's not a reason to not be in it. The consolidation is in the beginning. Patience is warranted here. You are going to have lots of opportunities to do lots of deals when we have DOL (Department of Labor) government-type regulation or a real bear market. We've been very disciplined in the deals we have done. The deals we are doing now are acqui-hires because of the talent. You can't just look at dollars and cents, you have to look at the capabilities you are getting. Every deal we have done so far, maybe we paid top dollar, but we've acquired great talent that came along with it. My message is be disciplined, be patient. The opportunity hasn't really started yet. We are not even in the first pitch of the first inning. If you can acquire talent and you need to acquire the company to do it, I think that is a really smart strategic move right now.

Q: Can you give me a sense of the type of deals you are working on?

A: If the owner is looking for a sunset, it most likely will be an all-cash deal. But all the deals are different.

Just this week, my team was discussing a way to standardize each deal, and I said, "Each owner has unique needs. It depends on where they are in their life." If it's a growth opportunity and you have a large advisory business and the cultural fit works, then there is a possibility of an equity swap. We want them to be financially rewarded if they are contributing to our success, but it also aligns our interests.

Q: Do you find (within your coaching community) that there are advisors that should be taking action on a continuity plan but fail to act?

A: Yes, Tom. It's actually heartbreaking. We have over five thousand advisors in our coaching community and over twenty thousand active alumni that know about Carson. There's not a week that goes by that there is not an unexpected death, and about 90 percent of the time, the value of the firm evaporates without a written plan. I just met a woman on the East Coast who had recently lost her husband due to a heart attack. He had a billion-dollar firm that she virtually got no value from. She said, "My husband told me he had a succession plan, but it was not in writing. It was a loose oral arrangement." [*emphatic*] And people count stuff like that as a succession solution. It's not.

Q: How would you describe a good succession plan?

A: The only way you really know is after you die. The second-best plan is to go to your best clients and say, "Here's my plan. If I died today, would you stay?" Early in my career, I thought I was well positioned with my succession plan. When I asked my top clients if they would stay, they said, "Hell no, we would be gone immediately." Since that time, I have created and refined a partnership around me for my succession plan.

You have to institutionalize the business or have a company that the clients are familiar with. That's why our partnership at Carson Partners is so powerful. Nothing has to change when the owner dies. No technology changes, no investment positions change, the client statements are the same. The client is just dealing with different people when the advisor dies or becomes disabled.

Q: What was the reason you decided to start your coaching program?

A: Tom, it was accidental. Because of my early success, people would ask to come visit me for a day and learn how I did things. I would often say, sure, come on out and spend some time and see how I do things. Soon after that, word spread throughout the industry, and I was really getting tied up. Pretty soon, it was turning into a full-time job. It was hurting my growth, and I started to formalize it. I started doing top producer workshops for a fee, and I learned through teaching—I became better. I would take notes on what new ideas were being presented by my peers and other attendees at our national Excel conference. I learned a tremendous amount from everyone that came into my coaching program. It really helped my growth. It was a cool, positive, virtuous cycle.

We just had our largest Excel conference ever in Chicago with over 1,300 attendees. The caliber of the advisor in our program has never been higher. It was completely by accident that I ended up in a coaching and consulting business. Your mind has to be open to learning from anybody. [Authors Note: Do you see how similar this is to the *Beginner's Mind* quote at the beginning of the introduction?] The older I get, the less I know, the more I'm open to fresh, new, and interesting information and ideas.

Q: Are there any new ideas or tools you can share with our readers?

A: Yes, there is an app called Blinkist. A real game changer. I have listened to two hundred or more books this year. And I also meditate. I've only been doing this for about three years now, but that has been a real game changer as well.

Just like the cycle of the farming seasons, Ron's life has gone full circle from farmer to financier to philanthropist.

Ron has planted many trees for financial advisors, and it's our turn to enjoy the shade while we continue to plant more trees for the next generation.

KEY ACTION STEPS/TAKEAWAYS

1. Surround yourself with great people. Be the librarian, not the library.

2. Succession (and continuity) plans should be discussed with both your team and your top clients and then written down in a formalized plan.

3. Add coaching programs at the top of your to-do list. You'll be surprised at how much you can learn from others. It can take you to places you never could have anticipated.

SUMMARY OF LESSONS LEARNED: HOW TO HACK THIS BOOK

———

"When you are content to be simply yourself and don't compare or compete, everybody will respect you."

—LAO TZU

I can almost guarantee this is not the ending you would expect to read in a book on financial services acquisitions.

But it is an ending you need to hear (or read) because it is best for you, your family, your employees, and your clients.

Before you get worked up about this philosophical ending, don't misinterpret what I am about to say.

Of course, I want you to be motivated to start a continuity or succession plan or finish one that has been lingering for way too long. Moreover, I want you to learn some great lessons from the talented people within these pages—lessons on how to grow, evaluate, and acquire practices, boutiques, or small businesses as Carolyn Armitage of ECHELON Partners describes in Chapter 6. I want you to play the long game and win by being proactive.

But you need to be mindful of who you are, your strengths and weaknesses, and know what your team is capable of achieving. You want to be "content to be simply yourself." Don't try to copy some big producers or aggregators unless you have a well-thought-out plan of action and a team to back up that plan. Conversely, don't be like a stick in the mud and say, "This is overwhelming, so I think I will stay put and do nothing." Don't end up at either extreme.

This is very important to grasp.

If you have the desire to be the best billion-dollar firm, then by all means go for it. If you are at $5 billion of AUM and want to grow to $10 billion in AUM, that would be a phenomenal accomplishment. The sky is the limit. Go for it.

But those goals are not for everyone. Nor should they be for everyone.

Throughout the past twenty years of acquisitions, I am astounded by the people I met who literally died from working too long or ignoring their health or both.

When Ron Carson told me of the owner of a successful billion-dollar RIA firm who recently died of a heart attack *without ever completing a written continuity or succession plan*, I knew then how I would end this book.

You see, it's not just about acquiring and growing, it's also about letting go, building for the next generation. By letting go and working on the next phase of your life, you actually encourage growth in your business. You play the long game when you let go. A famous Zen proverb says, "Let go or be dragged." Don't be dragged to your death!

I intentionally picked the opening quote to remind all of my readers that the lessons and insights in this book are not just about making money and growing AUM. It's about being yourself. Of course, we want to continue growing our firms and adding new clients and new capabilities. But one of my conclusions is that so many people are hearing about the need to grow that some may be rushing into this marketplace without being fully prepared, mentally *and* physically.

Another conclusion is that many advisors feel that if they are not at, say, $500 million in AUM, they are a failure or going nowhere. Moreover, if an advisor manages $5 billion, they may think, "Well, when I get to $10 billion, I will be happier and more confident."

I don't believe in that type of negative thinking or negative motivation. I think there is a much better way to look at this challenge. The best way is to look at the whole game of succession and continuity planning, along with M&A, as one huge opportunity to showcase your talents. This book has literally just scratched the surface of all the potential this market has to offer, so in summary, let's learn from the wisdom of all these experts.

Let's start with the most critical lesson first: culture.

LOCATION, LOCATION, LOCATION MEANS CULTURE, CULTURE, CULTURE

Almost everyone I know in business has memorized the three most important aspects of real estate: location, location, location. I now want you to mentally transfer that phrase into the M&A world as culture, culture, culture. All of the experts in this book, in one form or another, have emphasized this fundamental principle of cultural alignment.

In Chapter 2, Jeanie O'Reilly Northcutt reminds us that after the valuation is complete, "it's all about the fit." Find the right buyer (or seller) that matches or mirrors many of the strengths your firm currently has. David Grau also emphasized in the same chapter that even if you sell to a larger firm, make sure the culture is consistent with where you want to end up.

Dave DeVoe has his own take when he eloquently says that cultures need to "mesh" instead of "match." In his words, you *don't* want the seller and buyer to have identical cultures, because that may mean the seller isn't really ready to hand over the reins after all. DeVoe states that investment philosophy is easier to screen for, whereas cultural fit takes longer to evaluate.

Dan Kreuter addresses the culture challenge in his Five Elements of Power thesis. Staying power, along with brand and people power, help address the issue of culture, albeit in different ways. Staying power allows the seller to communicate to clients that the handoff to G2 has already started. The brand power implies that the new firm (whether an internal team took over or an external team bought you out) has an existing brand that can be tapped into. People power emphasizes the larger team and back-office support that *should* come with a successful transition.

Brett (not his real name), the CEO of a smaller broker-dealer, arrived at his new firm *specifically because* he had to help identify, create, and mold the new culture that management needed in order to grow effectively. As Brett stated, "We had autonomy but alignment." He was free to make changes that management both endorsed and supported.

In Chapter 10, my business coach Steve (not his real name) shared a story of a challenging acquisition. Steve was not involved in the deal itself, but he was acting as a referee of sorts for the buyer and seller. The key challenges were: culture clash, a disparity in business approaches, and personality conflicts.

The buyer and seller appeared to have a lot in common. They had the same back office, close physical proximity in the Midwest, and similar client demographics. However, the cultural differences made this a difficult acquisition. The buyer's practice was upscale and affluent, the seller's practice was middle-class and blue-collar. This is not a good fit.

Once again, culture played the biggest role in this challenging acquisition. It is no surprise that this transaction was difficult and burdensome.

Ron Carson has a great catchphrase that always resonates with me. "Culture eats strategy for lunch. The best strategies in the world will never be executed if you don't have a good positive, supportive culture."

From culture, we move on to the important topic of valuation.

VALUATION

Another key aspect of the M&A process is valuation. Whether you are buying, selling, or preparing an estate plan, it is important to arrive at some type of valuation for your practice or the practice you want to buy. Let's review what the experts have told us so far.

First and foremost, all the experts reiterated that you are buying cash flow and future growth. How you discount that cash flow and what growth rates you assume are important parts of the equation. Don't be shy about hiring the right accounting or consulting firms to run the numbers properly.

Terry Mullen, founder and CEO of Truelytics, reminds us that in his proprietary research, firms that planned for succession had higher performance scores and KPIs (key performance indicators) than those firms that did not. As you may recall, the next generation of his software can give you 24 KPIs after you input your zip code and answer seven basic questions about your practice. This is very similar to the Kelley Blue Book of the car industry.

DeVoe reminds us that there are over five thousand RIAs with over $100 million in assets. If our economy enters a prolonged recession and that coincides with a bear market, then valuations could drop drastically. You play the long game when you get your house in order, create a written succession plan, and are ready when these acquisition opportunities present themselves. Be ready for the Transition Tsunami.

James Hughes of Live Oak Bank shares with us that valuations for firms under $250 million might sell for three to five times EBITDA, whereas firms with over $1 billion in assets can trade for seven to ten times EBITDA. He also reminds us that the W2 model for compensation aligns the interests of the employees and advisors with those of the owners. This model is superior to the 1099 model that was the standard for a very long time.

Carolyn Armitage of ECHELON Partners reminds us that valuations only make sense in context. A firm for sale may be worth more to some buyers than others depending on the mix of clients, products, geography, and size. It is a mistake to focus on just one number in a vacuum. Remember that the more moving parts you have in your firm, the more challenging it is to find a buyer who can absorb all those parts.

Mike, who has owned a car wash in my town for over fifty years, has seen many business cycles. When he sees private equity money and other financing mechanisms flood the market, he always has concerns about valuation. This is eerily similar to what we are seeing in the current M&A market in financial services. Mike says, "They don't ever learn, these new buyers that come into our business every decade or so." He has witnessed firms coming in and overpaying for the car wash business and selling years later to someone else at a lower price. Although car washes are not the same as RIA or IBD firms, it still pays to listen to Mike's wisdom. After all, business cycles are still business cycles.

Valuation leads us to the key question: How do we keep the acquired revenue stream intact and growing? Answer: customer service.

CUSTOMER/CLIENT SERVICE

Even if you have the right culture and the proper valuation is agreed upon, you still need to make sure the team you have can take care of the most important asset of the firm: clients. I also use the word customers, because in Chapters 3 and 11, these nonfinancial industries don't use the word client but replace it with customer.

Dan Kreuter refers to people power as one of his Five Elements of Power that should accrue to any buyer in a transaction. This is especially true if you sell to a larger firm that has already systematized the client service aspect of the business.

When you create a team of service advisors that can act with authority but have alignment with top management, you create a runway that has unlimited potential.

You might recall that Tim Collins, the CEO of EBSCO, said, "Simply put, the universe within which EBSCO's discovery and access tools operate expands beyond our own servers. Customers are wanting seamless access and single sign-on for their users to access content no matter where that content resides." Once again, even though EBSCO is not a financial services company, they still have that value-added focus on the customer (client).

The idea of seamless access and a single sign-on is very similar to what many wealth management firms are trying to create and refine to compete in the twenty-first century. In the financial services industry, the idea of account aggregation has become commonplace, yet I can tell you that even today, firms that still struggle to make it easy for clients to have one access point for all of their financial information.

Mike Hurst has one of my favorite quotes of the whole book. "Basically, there are two kinds of people: those that do as much as they can, and those that do as little as they can get away with." Mike was always emphasizing the client-service experience. His philosophy on client service was very simple, very direct: "I would want to be for my clients what I would want someone to be for me. If I gave someone my money and something went wrong, I would want them to tell me what to do. And if there is an opportunity out there, I would hope the advisor would call me and say, 'Here is something to take advantage of.'"

Dan, the HR executive for the supply chain company Gazelle, also shared a simple customer service metric. As soon as the LOI was signed, Dan would proactively form an integration team. This integration team continues with some due diligence, but they also focus on the first hundred days after an acquisition.

Because sales volume was always the key metric in this industry, this is where the customer service role came into play. If the total sales *did not* decrease in the first hundred days after an acquisition, then that deal was considered a success. Dan's team would talk to every single customer, no matter how big or small, during the hundred-day transition period. This conversation had to be live—no emails, no text messages, no voice mails.

Dan's team was very focused on this step and would immediately forward any concerns and feedback to top management. This was in addition to the town hall meetings they would conduct with all new employees to ensure all questions were acknowledged and, if possible, addressed quickly.

Let's shift gears and talk about the character traits of our interviewees.

The next two topics, while equally important, touch more upon the personality traits and philosophical attitude of the CEO or advisor.

PERSEVERANCE

This might be the most obvious concept of the whole book, but you'd be surprised to know how many advisors I know who have given up on acquisitions because the first one or two didn't work out. The same scenario has happened with yoga and karate. I have met so many people over the years who started karate (or some other martial art) and gave up. The same with various styles of yoga. Yet invariably, each person would admit, "I wish I had stuck with it. It would have been so much better for me long term."

The same logic applies to our businesses and acquisitions in particular.

Let's review some of the best quotes and stories from our experts.

Terry Mullen never gave up. From his early twenties, he had a dream of running his own company, and all throughout his career, including the ups and downs, he stuck with it. He had ideas about selling bottled water way before it became a staple in our lives. From shoe companies to parking meters, Terry tried just about everything. Terry always embraced the concept of *kaizen*, or continuous improvement, throughout all stages of his career. We can learn a lot from people like Terry.

My karate instructor, Sensei Masataka Mori, had this to say to the tournament winners when presenting a trophy: "You won today because no one better showed up to beat you. Don't forget you must keep training for the long term. You must continue to train, to get better."

Never give up.

My martial arts story that you read in my introduction about the tournament loss in Los Angeles has a better ending. Although we did lose the *kumite* (fighting) part of the tournament, my team did win the kata (forms) part of the tournament. Even after losing one match, we came back and won a different type of match (team kata). We advanced to the world tournament in Japan and competed in team kata. We never gave up.

EBSCO founder Elton B. Stephens started selling magazines door-to-door during the start of the Great Depression just to pay for college. How could he have known, through his perseverance, that eighty-five years later his namesake firm would employ over six thousand people spread across twenty-five distinct businesses? You never know where you will end up playing the long game, but having the confidence to sell door-to-door, along with getting the US Army as a client, was certainly a good start.

He never quit, and he played the long game.

Ron Carson shared another classic quote during my interview when he stated, "You haven't failed until you quit trying."

You may recall the story of the farming crisis that changed the course of Ron's career. Because of this crisis in the early 1980s, Ron's parents went bankrupt when the FDIC took over the local banks. Ron adapted by changing careers into financial services as he morphed from farmer to financier. He never gave up.

TRAITS OF SUCCESSFUL ACQUISITIONS AND SUCCESSION PLANS

This entire book has been focused on preparing you for business acquisitions. The lessons below are *absolutely critical* for you to absorb and remember. These lessons can save you hundreds of hours and perhaps thousands of dollars if you pay attention to them. Remember, these are all live examples from real experts who have traveled, in some cases extensively, down the path of acquisitions or succession planning.

In Chapter 2, Jeanie O'Reilly Northcutt shared some important legal considerations. Don't sign *any* offer sheets until they are looked over by a competent attorney. Offer sheets are also known as letters of intent (LOI). These documents should normally be used *well before* a final purchase and sale agreement (P&S) is signed.

In Chapter5, Dan Kreuter reminded us, "M&A is really head-hunting on steroids. Instead of moving people, you move entire companies, and you have to be handy with spreadsheets, org charts, legal and compliance issues. You have to be a jack of all trades." Be prepared.

In Chapter 7, James Hughes told us that Live Oak Bank is now doing deals that are "positive cash flow from day one." With the right buyer and seller, the financing can be done up front, and this gives the credit-worthy buyer up to ten years to pay off the loan.

In Chapter 9, Mike Hurst told me that in 2011, one of his top executive clients blindsided Mike with a direct question about succession planning. Mike admitted he had never really thought of retirement, he just kept going to work, adding clients each year. Mike did his homework, never gave up, and after six years of meetings and false starts with other firms, he finalized his succession plan with my firm, Capital Wealth Management LLC.

Mike trusted his instinct and had to turn down many advisors who wanted a succession plan with him. Often other less reputable advisors tried to work with him without any signed agreements or even a memo of understanding, giving him some dodgy tax advice regarding IRS form 8594.

In Chapter 12, Ron Carson freely admitted, "My first M&A deal I ever did was a mistake. I didn't know what I was doing. I underestimated how critical culture is. It was somebody I didn't know that well, and they were a cultural misfit, and it created a lot of friction within my organization." Even the best sometimes make mistakes. But Ron adapted his approach and now says, "We spend an enormous amount of time now getting the culture right, and we've walked away from numerous deals because there was not cultural alignment."

One of the best quotes in an entire book of great quotes on the subject of acquisitions is: "The best deals you make are the (bad) ones you never do."

BEGINNER'S MIND AND THE TRUE PURPOSE OF ZEN

In my introduction, I shared with you these two critical topics because I wanted you to be aware of these concepts throughout the book. In my opinion, even if you have the right culture, the correct valuation, and a great client experience, that is not enough to continue growing and learning. Yes, perseverance is absolutely essential. Without it, little progress will be made. But you need more. You need to keep (or develop) a fresh mind and an open mind.

Do you have any concerns with your partners that you have not shared? Are you entirely on the same page as they are?

If those answers are yes followed by no, why not take a fresh approach and address these issues?

In terms of acquisitions, are there friends or contacts you should reach out to that might be a good fit for your firm? Have you called or emailed them? Why not? Are there wholesalers you can talk to regarding firms in your area that are good candidates to discuss succession planning? It is not enough to just talk about acquiring firms, you have to develop a plan of action to get in front of them. You must see things as they are, not as you want them to be.

Waiting around for a phone call is not a game plan. Ron Carson often says, "Hope is not a strategy."

Remember our Berkeley grad Dave DeVoe? He is referred to as an "RIA M&A Guru" by *Barron's* magazine. He hits the nail on the head as he describes the effort needed to participate in the M&A game.

"M&A takes a lot of time and energy," says DeVoe, "Whether you are on one side or the other and your ability to be more focused, more structured, and to identify the right candidates . . . this can really save everyone time and energy."

James Hughes and his employer, Live Oak Bank, demonstrate an excellent example of the beginner's mind concept. One of their first niche markets they wanted to conquer was loaning money to veterinarians. Because it was a new market for Live Oak, they took a unique approach and hired two veterinarians to assist in the underwriting of the loans. A fresh approach.

Once management saw that success, it didn't take too long before they shifted their focus to the financial advisor. Live Oak Bank saw an opportunity where others only saw risk. And Live Oak did this again and again, replicating a smart strategy.

Live Oak now has twenty-two different categories on their website under "Small Business Loans." Each new industry is an example of the beginner's mind concept. In the beginner's mind there are many possibilities.

You need to apply beginner's mind and the purpose of Zen to round out the lessons of this book. Once again, do not misinterpret what I am about to say. You don't have to take up martial arts, nor do you have to begin some daily practice of Zen or Buddhist meditation. Those are disciplines that help me tremendously in my career. That is my journey.

What you do need, in my opinion, is a way of cultivating or thinking that encourages a fresh look at what you are doing every day in your practice. This is the beginner's mind concept. For example, are there employees who have negative energy and take away from office morale? Are there clients that drag you (or your team) down? Why are these problems allowed to persist? Why not take action today? What is preventing you from doing what you need to do in order to create a better environment? The true purpose of Zen is to see things as they are. What are you not seeing?

THE DALAI LAMA

———

The Dalai Lama, when asked what surprised him most about humanity, said:

Man.

Because he sacrifices his health in order to make money.

Then he sacrifices money to recuperate his health.

And then he is so anxious about the future that he does not enjoy the present;

the result being that he does not live in the present or
the future;

he lives as if he is never going to die, and then dies having
never really lived.

SENSEI MASATAKA MORI OBITUARY

———

Born in 1932 in a small village in Fukuoka, Japan, Masataka
Mori grew up as the youngest child of Masanaga and Naoe
Mori. He was a rambunctious and popular child. He went
on to attend Takushoku University in Tokyo where he dis-
covered his great passion in life, karate. He became the team
captain of the Takushoku karate club. Upon graduating in
1955, he joined the Japan Karate Association (JKA).

In 1961, he met and married his lifelong partner, Keiko, and
within two years was sent by the JKA to Hawaii to teach at
the dojo there. Under his instruction, his Hawaii team made
history by defeating the all-Japan JKA team in competition.

His first daughter, Mayumi, was born in Hawaii during these years.

In 1968, he moved his family to New York City to become an instructor of JKA New York. His second daughter, Sayuri, was born shortly afterward. During the next fifty years, he would teach as Chief Instructor at the JKA dojo and colleges including Stony Brook University, City University of New York, Borough of Manhattan Community College, and the Columbia University karate club as well as at seminars and officiate at tournaments worldwide.

To him, karate was not a sport or about winning a competition but a lifelong discipline by which to develop one's character. He often said a person who practiced karate could contribute to society. Despite his advanced rank, he often taught beginners himself. He also enjoyed teaching children at his dojo and at the Japanese Children's Society, although he would often comment on how exhausting it was to keep the youngest ones on track. In 2011, he was awarded the rare ranking of ninth dan by the JKA. He loved teaching up to the end of his life; he participated in the July 2018 summer training camp in Connecticut.

He lived in Closter, New Jersey from 1978 on. When he was working, he was an avid golf enthusiast and a perfectionist gardener. In his later years, he enjoyed the company of his lively grandchildren and was known as *ojiichan*. He passed away on September 8, 2018, after having lived a full and wonderful eighty-five years.

Reprinted with permission from the Mori family.

GLOSSARY

1099 Form—The 1099-MISC or miscellaneous income form is an IRS form taxpayers use to report nonemployee compensation. This is generally a business payment—not a personal payment. Independent contractors, freelancers, sole proprietors, and self-employed individuals receive one from each client who paid them $600 or more in a calendar year.

AUM—Assets Under Management is the total market value of the investments that a person or entity manages on behalf of clients. Assets Under Management definitions and formulas vary by company.

BCP—Business continuity planning is the process involved in creating a system of prevention and recovery from potential threats to a company. The plan ensures that personnel and assets are protected and are able to function quickly in the event of a disaster. The BCP is generally conceived in advance and involves input from key stakeholders and personnel.

broker-dealer—A broker-dealer is a person or firm in the business of buying and selling securities for its own account or on behalf of its customers. The term broker-dealer is used in US securities regulation parlance to describe stock brokerages, because most of them act as both agents and principals. A brokerage acts as a broker (or agent) when it executes orders on behalf of its clients, whereas it acts as a dealer, or principal, when it trades for its own account.

CFP—A Certified Financial Planner is a formal recognition of expertise in the areas of financial planning, taxes, insurance, estate planning, and retirement. Owned and awarded by the Certified Financial Planner Board of Standards Inc., the designation is awarded to individuals who successfully complete the CFP Board's initial exams, then continue ongoing annual education programs to sustain their skills and certification.

EBITDA—Earnings before interest, taxes, depreciation, and amortization reflects a company's overall financial health and is sometimes more informative than looking at earnings or net income.. **financial advisor**—A general term that applies to a person who helps clients manage their money and helps secure their financial future. They may specialize in certain areas such as estate planning, budgeting, education planning, and insurance.

financial planner—A financial planner is one type of financial advisor who helps individuals and corporations meet their long-term financial objectives. Financial planners do their work by consulting with clients to analyze their goals, risk tolerance, life or corporate stages and identify a suitable class of investments for them. They may specialize in certain areas such as estate planning, budgeting, education planning, and retirement planning.

FPA—The Financial Planning Association is the principal membership organization for CERTIFIED FINANCIAL PLANNER™ professionals, educators, financial services providers, and students who seek advancement in a growing, dynamic profession. The primary aim of FPA is "to elevate the profession that transforms lives through the power of financial planning."

GDC—Gross dealer concession is the revenue to a brokerage firm when commissioned securities and insurance salespeople sell a product, whether it is an investment like stocks, bonds, mutual funds, or insurance like life insurance or long-term care insurance.

independent agent—An independent agent is an insurance agent that sells insurance policies provided by several different insurance companies rather than a single insurance company. An independent agent receives commissions for the policies that he or she sells and is not considered an employee of a specific insurance company.

investment advisor—An investment advisor is any person or group that makes investment recommendations or conducts securities analysis in return for a fee.

IPO—An initial public offering refers to the process of offering shares of a private corporation to the public in a new stock issuance. Public share issuance allows a company to raise capital from public investors. The transition from a private to a public company can be an important time for private investors to fully realize gains from their investment, as it typically includes share premiums for current private investors. Meanwhile, it also allows public investors to participate in the offering.

LOI—A letter of intent is a document declaring the preliminary commitment of one party to do business with another. The letter outlines the chief terms of a prospective deal. Commonly used in major business transactions, LOIs are similar in content to term sheets. One major difference between the two, though, is that LOIs are presented in letter format while term sheets are legalistic in nature.

M&A—Mergers and acquisitions is a general term used to describe the consolidation of companies or assets through various types of financial transactions, including mergers, acquisitions, consolidations, tender offers, purchases of assets, and management acquisitions. The terms are used interchangeably, but they have slightly different meanings. A merger is two firms of approximately the same size who join forces to move forward as a single new entity rather than remain separately owned and operated. However, when one company takes over another entity and establishes itself as the new owner, the purchase is called an acquisition.

OSJ—Office of supervisory jurisdiction. An OSJ branch must have at least one on-site supervisor who is a qualified and registered principal with the firm. The main office of each firm is always considered an OSJ and has supervisory jurisdiction and responsibility over all of the firm's non-OSJ branch offices.

P&S agreement—A purchase and sale agreement is a type of legal contract that creates an obligation for the purchaser to buy a product or a service and for the seller to sell the agreed-upon product or service. The agreement is sometimes referred to as a sales and purchase agreement, or SPA, or separately as a sales contract or purchase contract. The P&S agreement acts as a framework of a sale and provides a detailed outline of the transaction that will take place.

RIA—A registered investment advisor is a person or firm who advises high-net-worth individuals on investments and manages their portfolios. RIAs have a fiduciary duty to their clients, which means they have a fundamental obligation to provide investment advice that always acts in their clients' best interests. As the first word of their title indicates, RIAs are required to register either with the Securities and Exchange Commission (SEC) or state securities administrators.

succession planning—A strategy for passing on leadership roles—often the ownership of a company—to an employee or group of employees. Also known as "replacement planning," it ensures that businesses continue to run smoothly after a company's most important people move on to new opportunities, retire, or pass away. Succession planning can also provide a liquidity event enabling the transfer of ownership as a going concern to rising employees.

U4—The Form U4 is the Uniform Application for Securities Industry Registration or Transfer. Representatives of broker-dealers, investment advisors, or issuers of securities must use this form to become registered in the appropriate jurisdictions and/or self-regulatory organizations (SROs).

U5—The Form U5 is the Uniform Termination Notice for Securities Industry Registration. Broker-dealers, investment advisors, or issuers of securities must use this form to terminate the registration of an individual in the appropriate jurisdictions and/or self-regulatory organizations (SROs).

W2—The W2 form is the document an employer is required to send to each of their employees and the IRS at the end of the year. The form reports the employee's annual wages and the amount of taxes withheld from his or her paychecks.

wealth manager/wealth advisor—A wealth management advisor is a high-level professional who utilizes the spectrum of financial disciplines available—such as financial and investment advice, legal or estate planning, accounting and tax services, and retirement planning—to manage an affluent client's wealth for one set fee. A wealth manager often interacts with a client's attorney and CPA.

ACKNOWLEDGEMENTS

Thank you first and foremost to my family for supporting me through every step of the way, always.

When I began writing this book, I thought I had a robust knowledge of business acquisitions, but in keeping with the Zen-like theme of my book, I was reminded that knowledge is not static, and one must always be learning and improving themselves, especially with your passions. I am humbled by the response and support I received from friends and strangers alike. I have learned so much from you, and I hope that by sharing your expertise in this book, others may learn from you as well.

Thank to New Degree Press, Eric Koester, and Brian Bies for your patience and support throughout this process.

And thank you to everyone who: gave me their time for a personal interview, proofread drafts, pre-ordered the book to make publishing possible, helped spread the word to gather amazing momentum, and help me publish a book I am proud of. I am sincerely grateful for all your help. I could not have done this without you.

Carolyn Armitage	Amanda Brown
Carolyn Hine	Margaret Hine
Michael Nicoletti	Greg Opitz
James Bogart	Ron Carson
Charlotte Hine	James Hughes
Jeanie O'Reilly Northcutt	Erik Pahlow

Jason Carver

Rich Hunter

Ryan Porter

Linda Chamney

Michael Hurst

Tony Triano

Kelsey Conklin

Jim Hyre

Brian Winman

Chris Flint

Jonathan Jordan

Joel Worsfold

Kathy Frattaroli

Dan Kreuter

The DC 19 Group

Kelly Gallivan

Amanda Martin

Brian Bies

David Grau, Sr.

Carla McCabe

Professor Eric Koester

Doug Herrick

Kristen McGarry

Mark Herrick

Paul L. Merritt

Jordan Hickey

Terry Mullen

REFERENCES

INTRODUCTION:

Hine, T. and Brubaker, J. (2007). *NASD arbitration solution.* Hoboken, N.J.: John Wiley & Sons.

Suzuki, S. (2011). *Zen mind, beginner's mind.* Boston: Shambhala.

CHAPTER 1

Presentation Zen. (2011). *Fall down seven times, get up eight: The power of Japanese resilience.* [online] Available at: https://www.presentationzen.com/presentationzen/2011/03/fall-down-seven-times-get-up-eight-the-power-of-japanese-resilience.html [Accessed 8 Oct. 2019].

CHAPTER 2

BrainyQuote. (2019). *Bruce Lee Quotes.* [online] Available at: https://www.brainyquote.com/quotes/bruce_lee_413509 [Accessed 8 Oct. 2019].

CHAPTER 3

A-Z Quotes. (2019). TOP 25 QUOTES BY DOGEN (of 140) | A-Z Quotes. [online] Available at: https://www.azquotes.com/author/4029-Dogen [Accessed 8 Oct. 2019].

Quotefancy.com. (2019). Dōgen Quote: "One must be deeply aware of the impermanence of the world.". [online] Available at: https://quotefancy.com/quote/1165626/D-gen-One-must-be-deeply-aware-of-the-impermanence-of-the-world [Accessed 8 Oct. 2019].

Goodreads.com. (2019). Dōgen Quotes (Author of Moon in a Dewdrop). [online] Available at: https://www.goodreads.com/author/quotes/23358.D_gen [Accessed 8 Oct. 2019].

Haddon, H. and Jargon, J. (2019). Your Food Is Almost Here. *The Wall Street Journal.*

Olson, P. (2019). Amazon Bets on Meal Delivery. *The Wall Street Journal.*

Lieber, R. (2014). *Financial Advice for People Who Aren't Rich.* [online] Nytimes.com. Available at: https://www.nytimes.com/2014/04/12/your-money/start-ups-offer-financial-advice-to-people-who-arent-rich.html [Accessed 7 Oct. 2019].

PE Hub. (2018). *Palladin acquires Splash Car Wash - PE Hub.* [online] Available at: https://www.pehub.com/2018/11/palladin-acquires-splash-car-wash/ [Accessed 7 Oct. 2019].

Pcrp.com. (2019). Team |. [online] Available at: https://pcrp.com/team/ [Accessed 7 Oct. 2019].

CHAPTER 4

A-Z Quotes. (2019). Gautama Buddha Quotes About Moon | A-Z Quotes. [online] Available at: https://www.azquotes.com/author/37842-Gautama_Buddha/tag/moon [Accessed 8 Oct. 2019].

David Devoe: 3 M&A trends reshaping the industry. (2017). [video] Available at: https://www.investmentnews.com/section/video?playerType=Events&eventID=hdvest17&bctid=5490179440001&date=20170701 [Accessed 7 Oct. 2019].

DeVoe & Co. (2019). *Team — DeVoe & Co..* [online] Available at: http://www.devoeandcompany.com/team/ [Accessed 7 Oct. 2019].

RIABiz. (2019). *David DeVoe, Schwab's RIA M&A chief, leaves to start his own shop.* [online] Available at: https://riabiz.com/a/2011/11/21/david-devoe-schwabs-ria-ma-chief-leaves-to-start-his-own-shop [Accessed 7 Oct. 2019].

Garmhausen, S. (2019). *M&A Guru Dave DeVoe: Mega-RIAs Will Change the Game.* [online] Barrons.com. Available at: https://www.barrons.

com/articles/m-a-guru-dave-devoe-mega-rias-will-change-the-game-51548371254?redirect=amp [Accessed 7 Oct. 2019].

NFP (2019). *NFP to Acquire Bronfman Rothschild, Further Elevating Its Wealth Management Capabilities and Scale*. [online] Available at: https://nfp.com/about-us/news-perspectives/press-release-details/nfp-aquires-bronfman-rothschild-wealth-management [Accessed 7 Oct. 2019].

CHAPTER 5

Nihonshock.com. (2019). 29 Japanese Proverbs: Sep '09 Tweet Collection | nihonshock. [online] Available at: http://nihonshock.com/2009/10/japanese-proverbs-september-2009/ [Accessed 8 Oct. 2019].

Kreuter, D. (2019). *RIA Frenzy: What's Driving M&A*. [ebook] Available at: https://www.gstonellc.com/~gstonell/files/RIA%20Frenzy-%20What's%20driving%20M%26A.pdf [Accessed 7 Oct. 2019].

Musashi, M. and Bennett, A. (2018). *Complete Musashi*. La Vergne: Tuttle Publishing.

CHAPTER 6

A-Z Quotes. (2019). Confucius Quote. [online] Available at: https://www.azquotes.com/quote/62162 [Accessed 8 Oct. 2019].

CHAPTER 7

Goodreads.com. (2019). Osho Quotes (Author of Courage) (page 2 of 51). [online] Available at: https://www.goodreads.com/author/quotes/2856822.Osho?page=2 [Accessed 8 Oct. 2019].

CHAPTER 8

Goodreads.com. (2019). The Art of War Quotes by Sun Tzu. [online] Available at: https://www.goodreads.com/work/quotes/3200649-s-nz-b-ngf [Accessed 8 Oct. 2019].

CHAPTER 9

The Dōgen Institute. (2019). Dōgen Zenji. [online] Available at: https://dogeninstitute.wordpress.com/about/dogen-zenji/ [Accessed 8 Oct. 2019].

CHAPTER 10

Rimpoche, N. (2019). Anger and Patience. [online] Tricycle: The Buddhist Review. Available at: https://tricycle.org/magazine/anger-and-patience/ [Accessed 8 Oct. 2019].

CHAPTER 11

BrainyQuote. (2019). Confucius Quotes. [online] Available at: https://www. brainyquote.com/quotes/confucius_140548 [Accessed 8 Oct. 2019].

CHAPTER 12

Google.com. (2019). chinese quotes one generation - Google Search. [online] Available at: https://www.google.com/search?q=chinese+quotes+one+gener-ation&rlz=1C1SQJL_enUS811US811&sxsrf=ACYBGNQUmaucbz842RODub-gLKwKg8XlGyg:1570491782276&tbm=isch&source=iu&ictx=1&fir=nA-zWFEd-UtMtmM%253A%252CKOQq5kaLEohXAM%252C_&vet=1&usg=AI4_-kRL-TZImGXnt_U3FAnbBlxaLeQwSHg&sa=X&ved=2ahUKEwiRjLjmqYvlAhX-shOAKHeuzCjEQ9QEwBX0ECAcQDA#imgrc=nA-zWFEdUtMtmM: [Accessed 8 Oct. 2019].

Wiseoldsayings.com. (2019). Chinese Proverb Quotes and Sayings | Wise Old Sayings. [online] Available at: http://www.wiseoldsayings.com/authors/chi-nese-proverb-quotes/ [Accessed 8 Oct. 2019].

HOW TO HACK THIS BOOK

Goodreads.com. (2019). A quote from Tao Te Ching. [online] Available at: https://www.goodreads.com/quotes/13401-when-you-are-content-to-be-simply-yourself-and-don-t [Accessed 8 Oct. 2019].

DALAI LAMA QUOTE

Google.com. (2019). dalai lama quote on man and health - Google Search. [online] Available at: https://www.google.com/search?rlz=1C1SQJL_enU-S811US811&biw=1904&bih=928&tbm=isch&sxsrf=ACYBGNRPRiqfVlWVwzidh_mk5efNcrPcOg%3A1570493496146&sa=1&ei=ONSbXZHOCMK5ggeLoY2YCw&q=dalai+lama+quote+on+man+and+health&oq=dalai+lama+on+man&gs_l=img.1.2.0j0i8i30l2j0i24.137926.143617..146205...1.0..2.88.3284.48......0....1..gws-wiz-img.....7.35i39j35i362i39j0i67._gWMPTZkl2s#imgrc=PD-V3dgCF3hnmM: [Accessed 8 Oct. 2019].

GLOSSARY

Investopedia. (2019). Investopedia. [online] Available at: https://www.investo-pedia.com/ [Accessed 8 Oct. 2019].

Made in the USA
Middletown, DE
09 September 2020